Date Due

MAR 2 3 1965			
APR 4			
DEC 21 75			
APR 9 '76			
MAR 5			
MAY 1			

Demco 293-5

MAJESTY AND MISCHIEF

Books by William S. White

THE TAFT STORY

CITADEL: The Story of the U.S. Senate

MAJESTY AND MISCHIEF

William S. White

MAJESTY &

MISCHIEF

A Mixed Tribute to

F.D.R.

McGRAW-HILL BOOK COMPANY, INC.
NEW YORK   **TORONTO**   **LONDON**

For June

Foreword

The scheme and the purpose of this book may need some brief explanation, and perhaps some disclaimer. It is in truth and by fixed intention a subjective reckoning, a recollection of the past primarily as a base for a commentary on the consequences, good and bad, of that past. The aim has been to provide a *personal* estimate and assessment, by a man who lived through that past and was at most points in intimate touch with it as a journalist, of the impact of Franklin D. Roosevelt upon many things: This world, this country, its politics in general, its party structures, its social realities and its human conditions.

It is thus not a work of research or of history-by-footnote. As to research, I set out in the beginning to do much; I found, early on, that for this book it was not research that I needed or wanted. Like most men I have read a good deal of Rooseveltiana over the years. All of this has no doubt influenced me in one degree or another and at one time or another. What is written here, however, is simply out of my own mind and—not too infrequently, to use a rather sticky term—out of my own heart. But as will be seen in the text, I have talked directly to, or had correspondence with, a good many personages who had connection with FDR.

To the best of my knowledge and belief nothing has come from traditional bibliographical sources, with these exceptions: A few facts from James F. Byrnes' *All in One Lifetime* and *Speaking Frankly;* a moving aid to my own memories of the Roosevelt death in rereading William Hassett's *Off the Record with FDR;* a kind of intellectual communion, over the years, with Chester Wilmot's *The Struggle for Europe;* a grateful reading of Mario Einaudi's *The Roosevelt Revolution.*

Wilmot's views of Roosevelt's and Churchill's wartime differences, looking to the post-war period, had in fact from the beginning been substantially my own. As a war correspondent I was accredited to British forces as well as American forces before and after D-Day, and so I had a fairly "inside" view of British strategic policies and aims.

Finally, I am deeply obliged to many eminent men—President Kennedy, Vice President Lyndon Johnson, Former Vice President Nixon, Adlai Stevenson, Henry Wallace, Francis Biddle, Archibald MacLeish, among them—for talking frankly and most helpfully to me, most of them in person, a few of them by letter.

It should be made very clear, however, that I alone am responsible for all conclusions, estimates, errors, and notions in this book.

William S. White

Washington, April, 1961.

MAJESTY AND MISCHIEF

Chapter

One

The strong old man sat absolutely still as he looked out into the gathering darkness of that April day. His right hand was in a half-fist, though it did not move at all; tears stood on his round, heavy face. "Now," he said softly, as though only to himself, "now the sons of bitches will start trying to dance all over his grave. Well, by God, let them try!"

The old man put a stubby pen into an inkwell and then slowly scratched out a statement for the press. This was the moment, on April 12, 1945, when the Speaker of the House of Representatives, Sam Rayburn of Texas, was accepting the fact that the thirty-second President of the United States had just died in Warm Springs, Georgia.

It was far more than this; it was a moment when the most extraordinary period in our history had come to a sudden, jolting end, without warning to this country or to the wide world, with the last heartbeat of Franklin Delano Roosevelt. Neither his people nor the Allied peoples had known that he was in any way seriously ill; there had been so much dying in so many places for so long that the obvious fact of his own "expendability" (this was one of those coldly precise terms that the Second World War had added to the common language even of schoolboys) had hardly been reckoned with anywhere.

Every sentient man and woman now at the age of maturity,

or beyond that age and, so, into the age of recollection and on personal terms with the approach of personal death, will have his own remembrance of that April day. My own memories will best serve, for the moment, my own purposes. I was then a Congressional correspondent for *The New York Times* and had only lately returned from long service in the European Theater of Operations as an assault war correspondent. Now my life had been altered—oddly and suddenly altered and, in my own case, softened too much, too soon by a sudden return to civilian pursuits. It was a long way from reporting actions with the First Division in the edge of Germany to reporting actions on the floors of the Senate and House. And I had known so much death in so many places—British death, American death, Polish death, German death—that I had thought the phenomenon to have been forever and overly familiarized in my mind.

So, on this day in April, bored with my circumstances and not much interested in whatever debates had been going on earlier in the afternoon in Congress, I walked idly from the Senate chamber through unlit corridors across to the House side. As I approached Rayburn's small private office—known then, as now, as "the Board of Education," where he met his friends for a late afternoon drink—a compact, brisk and not vastly impressive man was hurrying away, clapping a fairly large white hat on his head. I knew this man only by sight; his name was Harry S. Truman. He was from Missouri. And, though many had forgotten it and he on his part had never sought to assert his position, he was also the Vice-President of the United States.

In a pool of darkness near the elevator shaft just outside the Board of Education stood an old friend, tall but now somehow crumpled, as though the vertical bones had suffered some odd collapse. I stopped to talk with him. His black hair was mussed across his forehead; his tie was askew; he looked, in fact, very much like a man who had had far too much to drink, though this was not at all the case. He came out of the darkness and reached out both his hands. "*He's* dead. *He's* dead," said this friend, who was then a Congressman, a man named Lyndon B. Johnson. "*He* was always like a daddy to me."

So we stood there for several moments. At last I turned away, saying nothing, really, and feeling, for the moment, little more. Then I remembered having seen the President not long before, from a seat upstairs in the House Press Gallery, perhaps a hundred feet directly upward from where Johnson and I had just been standing. I remembered how worn—and somehow broken—Franklin D. Roosevelt had looked when, just a few days ago, he had sat in a large chair on the dais of the House reporting to a joint session of Congress on an Allied conference that had taken place at a little, immensely far-off place, somewhere on the Black Sea. Yalta it was.

I remembered that never before had FDR allowed weariness or illness—not even the endless weariness of a man who for twenty-odd years had been a cripple—to tempt him to do anything other than stand painfully and exactly erect at every public occasion of every kind. I remembered the lines in a face that had no longer been handsome. I remembered all the years that had gone, the Depression, the wild, wonderful (and sometimes faintly crackpot) remedies for it; the slow, terrible march of events that had led to a thousand rumors of war and then to the fact of war itself, war all over the world, the lights turned down all over the world, the incredible encompassing of events of horror and grandeur in so short a span of years. I remembered the past gallantries, the past and still undying bitterness, the outflowing courage of an indomitable man who had somehow identified himself with, and made himself one with, all that had been struggle and high endeavor and hope all over the world. And suddenly I, who had felt too little, now felt too much. It seemed not simply that a Man of History had died; but that history itself had lost its attribute of immortality, that history itself had died, in a little town I had never seen, a little town in Georgia called Warm Springs.

It was a kind of grief, both personal and institutional, that I had never known and would never know again. It was one of the unspeakable memories of wartime, unique, never to change and never to end, forever imprinted upon mind and heart rather like the remembrance of the English Channel on the night before D Day, when one knew that, whatever later might happen or not happen, nothing one ever later knew or sensed would be like this moment when time itself parted like a broken rope. This death was an unbridgeable, an irreparable point of breakage between past and future. This was the end of glory and maybe even of hope, the most utterly final end that one would ever see.

So I turned the doorknob and went into the room where Rayburn sat, so unmoving and so alone—as Roosevelt himself had been alone, but for members of his staff, when death had overturned him in the cottage in Warm Springs long before his work was done. Rayburn's eyes could not reject his grief; the tears he could not halt or control. But his mind, the tough mind of a good political man (his chief, FDR, had had the even tougher mind of a great political man), this was something else again. His mind, even at this very onset of the news, refused the sad preoccupations with the past which his emotions thrust upon him as the air of a funeral hymn will break insistently if softly upon, and below, senses directed entirely elsewhere. No, the Rayburn mind went, instinctively and instantly, to where Roosevelt's mind itself would have gone in other circumstances: to a sudden, instinctive assaying both of the legacies that had been left by the great man's life and attitudes and policies—and also to the bills that would now be presented for payment. These would be a series of payments running through all the years to come, to those who had simply hated him, to those who had honorably opposed him, and to those who had suffered from what he had done as others had been saved by what he had done.

It was not merely the fact that an ending had come, but that it had come so rudely, so without notice and so without time for any kind of transition. The future had been brusquely opened before the moving present or even the past had been allowed by fate to come to any rational halt or close. The glory had died with Roosevelt—the glory for his party, certainly; for his government, very probably, as then it looked; and for the Allied world, absolutely and positively, as then it seemed. But the power remained. Constitutionally, it was in the hands of the undistinguished, blocky man who had just, a few minutes before, put on his white semi-Western hat and left in a hurry to go to the White House. But where would it, where *could* it, now reside in fact? Who on earth could hope to finish the inspired, often chaotic symphony in public and world affairs which the master musician had been forced harshly to put down in a world wounded and broken —and which he had put down without leaving so much as a handful of scattered thematic notes to indicate the ultimate design?

This man who remained so unmoving in the Board of Education, this ornery old cuss (as they would have said in Texas) who would not admit his sorrow past his heavy eyelids, had thrust a blunt finger of thought upon the heart of the matter: What was going to happen, now, to the American Republic? He thought first of his party (and, indeed, so would Roosevelt have done), for his party was an inseverable part of his country, an arm to its torso, or—as a good partisan like

Rayburn would reckon it—the true brain above its whole trunk. And in his anguish, an anguish compounded of love for a great and powerful friend now departed, for a system and for a nation and for all its associated and allied nations, he had spoken with more harshness than was really in his heart. He did not mean that all of "them," the opposition, were really "sons of bitches." He meant that some of them were, at least in this moment of his own overpowering sadness and loss. And he knew that, before nightfall, some of these would be heard publicly to proclaim their satisfaction at the departure, forever, of that so-and-so in the White House. But most of all the real, inner anxiety was for the continuity of the United States of America, that strange, mixed, callous and sentimental, heedless and cautious, silly and grave, selfish and selfless, stupid and wise, multifaced organism which the dead President had so chivvied and jollied, frightened and reassured, measured and remeasured, torn up and remolded, through years of urgencies of a kind not before precisely visited upon mankind.

But as this mourning but still thinking man, Rayburn, rose at last, wordless now for many minutes, and snapped off the last light in his office and walked slowly away, currents of great meaning were moving all over the United States and all over the world. It was true that before this, in our life as a nation, we had suffered the sudden and awful shock of the leader's death. In many minds there rose at once the recollection of Abraham Lincoln struck down in an evil *non sequitur* of history by the hand of a man motivated by only an enfevered emotional rubbish just as Lincoln was at last bringing to its close the measureless tragedy of our War Between the States. The parallel, however, was surely thin. An enfeebled nation, it is true, had depended upon Abraham Lincoln. But now it was a sick world—and a world of far deeper and more sophisticated sicknesses where millions alive would have been better dead—that had been left bereft. The fact that Roosevelt was killed not by a man but by an impersonal thing, a cerebral hemorrhage, was surely an apt act of destiny. For all personal things, including the suffering bodies of that most personal of all things, the human creature, had taken on new meanings in the space from Appomattox to Aachen and Bastogne. There was now so much of everything, of exertion, of terror, of loss, of gain, of unexampled dilemma, of infinite peril, that human tortures had taken on not merely new degrees but new principles. It would have been the grossest of improprieties, the gauchest violation of the inherent logic of the fitness of things, for Franklin D. Roosevelt to have been driven from this fantastic arena by the mere hostile muscular motion of a single man.

Still, as the news spread that evening and night, and while sorrow moved across this and many lands and small, gasping eulogies were said by housewives sitting under hair-drying cones and solemn salutes were issued by statesmen in many capitals, something else was spreading, too. This was a kind of slow osmosis of awareness, instinctive at first, that what had always gone forward before, the government of the United States, must and would somehow and after all go forward still. How well it would go on was another matter.

Chapter

Two

The man in the white hat had by now picked up, if in clumsily humble hands, some of the scattered fragments of leadership that had fallen wide and lifelessly on the spring air when life had left the other man down at Warm Springs in Georgia. Truman had gone down to the White House in answer to a summons from Stephen Early, the Roosevelt press secretary, not knowing what was afoot. He had left Rayburn's office—the Board of Education—supposing that he was being called down simply because Roosevelt had unexpectedly returned to Washington and wanted to talk about something quite minor. (Mr. Truman had never been overburdened by invitations to the White House; "the Boss" had not regarded him as an overly significant figure and indeed had rarely talked to his Vice-President about anything of real importance.)

But when Harry Truman arrived at 1600 Pennsylvania Avenue, walking in with that shyness and self-depreciation he had always shown toward that place and its magnificent tenant, FDR, he was taken with unusual gravity to Mrs. Roosevelt's study. Eleanor Roosevelt was quiet, tearless and absolutely poised. She put her hand on Truman's shoulder and said to him, softly and plainly and directly: "Harry, the President is dead." It was about 5:30 in the afternoon; Mr.

Truman's mind does not now fix the time any more precisely than that.

He stood silent for a second or two, trying to keep from crying and trying, also, to place himself in this scene, to find reality in a world of sudden unreality. Then he asked Mrs. Roosevelt what he could do for her. She replied: "No, no, *Mr. President,* tell us what *we* can do. Is there any way we can help *you?*" She had just told Early and Admiral Ross T. McIntire, FDR's physician, "I am more sorry for the people of the country and the world than I am for us."

Mrs. Roosevelt might well have added that she was sorry, too, for Harry S. Truman. During that part of his fourth term which he had been able to serve, Roosevelt had been in the United States hardly more than an aggregate of a month and Truman had not been taken into his confidence in any important way even in those brief days.

At any rate, the Missouri "machine politician" now stared sadly and all but uncomprehendingly at Mrs. Roosevelt—and at a future confronting him with a brightly malicious grimace at his own unavoidable lack of preparation for the immense job now thrust upon him. But he took up his burden sturdily. His first instinct was to pray—for himself and for the strength and wit to do what he knew in only the vaguest way he would now have to do. His rather rustic, but genuine, Baptist faith required prayer of him.

Crowds already were gathering in somber silence across the street from the White House, in Lafayette Square. These for the most part were what writers so like to call "ordinary people"—as though only "ordinary people" could somehow sanctify a proceeding the decency of which would otherwise be inevitably suspect. But not then (and not later) in that park were those standing and waiting, for something they knew not quite what, altogether and in every case ordinary people. One who stood there later, reflectively and with a sense of elegy not unmixed with a coolly critical if unbitter view toward the fallen President, was a man named Nelson Rockefeller. For him a future of honors and power was even then slowly opening up in this time of the thrust of a thousand changes.

"Ordinary man." "Common man." These terms, these slogans, in some strange, almost telepathic, way sprang at once to the minds of people. Their curious impact, their strange weight, might well have been felt through the very windows of the White House on that dark evening by Harry Truman himself, who had come to see a President and found, instead, that *he* was a President. Harry Truman was instantly elected to be this "common man," this "ordinary man."

The first thing he did was to order a government airplane put at the disposal of Mrs. Roosevelt. The next thing he did was to call "Mama," Mrs. Bess Truman, and his daughter, Margaret, and ask them to come at once to the White House. Then he telephoned Harlan Fiske Stone and asked the Chief Justice to come and swear in the new President. He summoned the members of the Roosevelt Cabinet as well. A Bible was found with some difficulty in the White House, which in the exigencies and alarms of the war had become more and more a purely official residence and less and less a home. The Roosevelt sons were spread about in the far theaters of war. And while Franklin Roosevelt had been complaining of "a terrific headache" and passing almost immediately into unconsciousness and then death in Georgia, Mrs. Roosevelt had been attending a meeting of the Thrift Club—one of the endless series of good works endlessly looked after by this good lady—at the Sulgrave Club on Dupont Circle in Washington.

For Truman, "the lightning had struck," or, as he put it to a group of reporter friends: "Boys, if you ever pray, pray for me now. I don't know whether you've ever had a load of hay fall on you, but when they told me yesterday what had happened I felt like the moon, the stars and all the planets had fallen on me. I've got the most terribly responsible job a man ever had."

To me long, long later—long after he himself had had his own hour in the White House and had retired with stout *élan* unimpaired—Mr. Truman put it this way. "Of course I was very much disturbed when I heard that he was dead and that I was then President; I had a great many things to think about, and I did the best I could with all of them."

It was very dark by the time he had taken the oath of office with his hand on the Bible that had been so elusive. But this was a time when night was not night, except in the hearts of so many; all over Washington and all over the country the lights burned without ceasing. The air was full of the words of sorrow, from a million face-to-face conversations and from an unending series of radio broadcasts. I remember the scene in which I myself happened to be, the Washington office of *The New York Times.* The acting news editor of the bureau, Robert F. Whitney, had loved Roosevelt with the unuttered fondness of a shy and little-speaking man. All of us on the writing staff went to work, without a word to Whitney or each other, on this or that aspect of the President's death.

The chief of the bureau, Arthur Krock, had carried on a feud for years with FDR, a feud based as much on personal misunderstandings as on Krock's lively skepticism toward the New Deal as a matter of political conviction and principle. Many, many people, particularly those who had idolized Roosevelt, would have been a bit tense that night had they known that the main story of his death was being written by Arthur Krock.

As a columnist, he had found so much to criticize, and so often, that it would have been understandable to expect something rather chill on this occasion. But Krock is a big man (and the Roosevelt era had encouraged what was big in men, even big hatreds, and rather discouraged what was petty and small). So Krock went to his typewriter impassive of face if faintly hurried in demeanor. What he produced would shame no man:

"The President, stricken by a cerebral hemorrhage, passed from unconsciousness to death on the 83rd day of his fourth term and in an hour of high triumph. The armies and fleets under his direction as Commander in Chief were at the gates of Berlin and the shores of Japan's home islands . . . and the cause he represented and led was nearing the conclusive phase of success. . . . The democratic process has never had a greater shock."

And this word, the word "shock," more nearly than any other expressed the national mood all that night, and for many days ahead. The new occupant of the White House was peering into the surrounding darkness no less than were many other of the world's eminent men.

The man who but for Truman would now himself have been President, Henry A. Wallace, had been in a dentist's chair when he received, over the radio, word of the President's death. Wallace, who had been rather absently dumped by Roosevelt (through others) as Vice-President in 1944 to make way for the more "solid" Truman, was now a less-than-enchanted Secretary of Commerce instead. The single word "shock" is the sole descriptive word he has used to me in trying to recall, from a distance of sixteen years, what had passed through his mind then: "The only impression was one of shock. . . . When we [the Cabinet] gathered together for the swearing-in of President Truman that was the only impression [shock] I remember from the attitude of the others."

It was really more, of course, than merely shock. For Truman was the usurper, in Wallace's mind, and he was the "peanut politician from Kansas City" in many another and less emotionally committed mind. He began quickly, if imperceptibly, to move into a mastery of a Cabinet which was far less than in awe of him. At first, he declared over and over to those about him that his one purpose in life and in office would be to do, unquestioningly and in every case, precisely what FDR would have done. It was, of course, an unwise and an extreme and an oversentimental loyalty. (Truman's convictions for extreme loyalty would make him, in criminal court terminology, a seven- or eight-time loser, at least.) For it was an era itself, not only a man, that was dead, and it was before long borne in upon even Truman himself that this was so. The increasing Truman mastery of the Cabinet commenced with this recognition on his part. And it moved with accelerated speed as he began to divest himself, one by one, of those Roosevelt associates who were either too intractable (exit Wallace and James F. Byrnes of South Carolina) or simply too humanly close to the long and persistent shade of FDR (exit Francis Biddle).

From one point of view, Wallace and Byrnes simply could not be maintained in office for the simple reason that neither thought Truman was or ought to be really President. Each had been denied in the 1944 Democratic convention—Wallace thrust from the Vice-Presidency he had already held and Byrnes refused the vice-presidential nomination he believed he had earned and had thought Roosevelt intended to bestow. Each of these disappointed men would set out at once to direct for "the little man from Missouri" the foreign policy which, manifestly in the view of each, he himself was incompetent to direct.

Byrnes's first thought, when he learned of the President's death, was of a remark General Lucius D. Clay had made to him not long before. "He will not live long," Clay had said of Roosevelt, thus expressing bluntly the amazed distress he had felt upon seeing FDR after long absence and thus becoming aware of how much he had altered. Byrnes, as he later informed me, thought at the time that Clay was unnecessarily worried—"The President had remarkable recuperative powers; he seemed to be made of rubber and would bounce back in a short time."

But Byrnes's next thoughts were two wholly separate ones: of the incalculable mass of "unfinished business" that had been left in the White House, and of the surpassingly strange mixture FDR had been in the eyes of this South Carolinian who had served a President who both repelled and fascinated him.

Byrnes later remembered Roosevelt first and always as a politician, both imaginative and conservative; full of good purposes but quite ready to use other men to the last ounce by playing "upon their weaknesses, vanities and prejudices. To him men were so many tools to be used for the accomplishment of what he believed to be a good purpose." But then Byrnes "forgot his weaknesses and thought only of the remarkable qualities that had enabled him to inspire the free peoples of the world to unite in defense of freedom, and to mold the energies of America so that its might brought victory to the Allied cause."

From the moment Roosevelt died it was fated that the Wallaces and the Byrneses alike would have to depart from the high public life of the Democratic Party. The Wallaces were too undisciplined, too automatically and ecstatically "liberal," to be useful in any successor regime. For FDR had been able to use them, much as Byrnes himself put it in his epitaph, mainly because FDR himself wore the highest crest of liberalism and so could casually restrain and canalize the knee-jerk liberalism of the Wallaces by a mere laugh and wave of his hand. FDR could be liberal when he wanted to be; he could turn it on and off. And the Byrneses—the Southern Bourbons whom more and more James Francis Byrnes had come to typify—were historically incongruous even in the Roosevelt era. That they had maintained representation in the power structure throughout that era was explainable most of all simply by the fortuitous and illogical fact that here, too, FDR was able to restrain and to canalize their incipient or actual right-wingism. Truman had no built-in approval of the liberals, the genuine ones or the professional ones, and no built-in approval either from the Old South, which had accepted from Roosevelt federal policies that it would not soon accept again from any President.

But Wallace and Byrnes personally had to go, after only brief services in the Truman years, for yet another reason: They had been really *powerful* in the Roosevelt years. And the towering, the overmastering, the central fact, was that the new Presidency could not simply go on as a mere slow liquidation of the old Presidency. For this, as Truman knew from instinct and also from history (of which in his unobtrusive way he had read much), would shortly mean that there could be no Presidency at all.

Biddle, for his part, had to go most of all for the reason that one must at last not only clear away all the funeral chairs but one must also say firm goodbye to those whose continued presence would sustain the dead man's image forever in one's sitting room.

Biddle was not so much a powerful member of the Roosevelt Administration as a member specially and humanly *close*, in the sense of a shared social class and a common private way of life, to the late President. He left the Cabinet with a sense of irony; but, as he once told me, he found in time that the distaste and dislike he had felt for the new President had given way to quite different feelings—affection and great admiration. He remained in the Democratic Party, the jerry-built, crazily illogical structure of a party that Roosevelt had somehow put together and made to work. But Byrnes and Wallace left more than public office; they left their party after Roosevelt had left it in death; or, rather, after the party itself, as he had made it, collapsed and fell. For the party he had put together with a unique kind of personal cement had life no longer once life had left his own body at Warm Springs. Its center remained; this center had been there before FDR. But the wings fell off and away—into a leftward void with Wallace and his kind, into a rightward void with Byrnes and *his* kind.

Chapter

Three

On this evening of the death of the old President and the tremulous installation of the new, most of the fallen President's great colleagues about the world were, like men of Rayburn's stamp here at home, filled not simply with shock but also with thought and foreboding. Churchill (he was "Mister" Churchill then, and not Sir Winston) did what anyone who knew him would have known he would do. With the spare punctilio and decorum of the old school, he put himself into seclusion. And what he thought there, no one, not even Mrs. Churchill, will ever surely know.

Then, having spent a night of due and proper silence, he cabled to Mrs. Roosevelt:

"I send my most profound sympathy in your grievous loss. It is also the loss of the British nation and of the cause of freedom in every land.

"I feel so deeply for you all. As for me, I have lost a dear and cherished friendship which was forged in the fire of war. I trust you may find consolation in the glory of his name and the magnitude of his work."

The King's court went into a seven-day period of mourning.

The German radio had long turned toward this man Roosevelt, the author of "unconditional surrender," a special venom. Now it declared that Roosevelt would "go down in history

as the man upon whose instigation the present war turned into
the Second World War. . . . The President of the United
States, after all, attained only one thing: In his own camp
he lifted the strongest competition into the saddle—the Bol-
shevist Soviet Union."

The Nationalist Chinese leader, Chiang Kai-shek, was at
breakfast when the news came. He was unable to eat, and
he went at once into solitude. Circumstances, the march of
history, fate or destiny, all these forces were preparing to
make of this thin, shaken, futile generalissimo an instrument
in the hands of Roosevelt's enemies and of the enemies of his
party. Chiang's vast, corrupt, hopeless, powerless country
with its 600,000,000 people was at length to pass to Communist control. And Roosevelt, and Truman after him, were
at length to be blamed in passionate partisan rhetoric—and
savage nonsense—for this disaster of so massive a malignancy.
Nationalist Chiang was to fall because Chiang was not strong;
Nationalist China was to fall because Nationalist China could
not or would not fight effectively. But the very words
"China" and "Chiang Kai-shek" were to become the symbols
for an evil American failure, or worse. And China itself was
to become, in Red control, a faceless horror, an illimitable
pit of universal slavery that would make even the Soviet
Union look almost a genial land.

Charles de Gaulle of France, who had much reason to
dislike FDR but much more reason to venerate him, cleared
his mind for the moment of memory of the sharp words he
had exchanged with and about this American during the war.
To both Roosevelt and Churchill, De Gaulle had been a
prickly plant, indeed, a man of such haughty self-confidence
as to make either of these powerful and happy egos seem as
timid as a schoolgirl at her first dance. Now, De Gaulle
dressed himself with meticulous care for a mission of regal

sorrow—a sorrow which was very real; for De Gaulle, too, was a big man. He gathered up the French Foreign Minister, Bidault, and they went to the American ambassador in France, Jefferson Caffery, to express France's feelings. "It is a terrible loss," said De Gaulle, "not only for our country and me personally but also for all humankind." "A great disaster!" cried Bidault.

The hulking, enigmatic, suprabureaucratic machine in the Kremlin was cranked up that night and at length out came the regrets of a man called Josef Stalin—and no doubt sincere regrets, too, as far as they went; for Stalin had found in the gay and essentially trusting Roosevelt a sympathy which old Churchill never even pretended lay in him.

This, remember, was a day of great and terrible events in many places, quite outside Washington and quite outside the lofty echelons in which the great war leaders moved. One of those down in the tiers below, a fellow called Harold Macmillan, was—like many another—too pressed with what he was doing under forced draft at the time even to be able to remember later just what he was doing and where he was doing it. To an inquiry I sent to 10 Downing Street, the residence of British Prime Minister Harold Macmillan, I received a note saying this, in part: "The Prime Minister does not recall where he was on the 12th April 1945, though he thinks he was in Caserta. Nor does he recall the circumstances in which he heard of Mr. Roosevelt's death. I hope that the absence of this piece of information does not embarrass your researches unduly. . . ."

Caserta and the whole of the North African-Mediterranean bridge to the world over which Axis and Allies had struggled so violently was ever in the mind of this and every other Briton. The Nile was no farther from their thoughts than the Rhine. For Britain, under the lash of a brilliantly inventive

but nevertheless tradition-stored Churchillian mind, was fighting the Second World War from imperial London with
purposes rather different and strategic views far different from
those with which FDR had been fighting it from a curiously
parochial quasi-Southern town called Washington, D. C., now
changed by events into the unready bursting capital of the
Allied world. Macmillan's task was then, and long had been,
this, as a diplomatic representative nominally of King George
VI but actually of Winston Churchill: to help move aside all
obstacles—not excluding, for example, the occasional stiff
haughtiness of General Charles de Gaulle—to the ultimate success of a British policy of warfare which looked coldly beyond
the inevitable V Days to the shape of the world of the future.

The task was not so much to make sure that the sun never
set on the British Empire; for this would have been quite
beyond the self-confidence even of Churchill's England. But
the task was at least to make sure that the sun did not rise
on a new world, after war's darkness had lifted, in which
Soviet power had supplanted Western power, a world in
which a thing called Fascism had been destroyed only to leave
a thing called Communism spreading westward through the
ancient lands of the Near East and Balkan Europe. The far-
removed Roosevelt, in short, had not been in any intimate way
a part of Macmillan's war: *His* main point of contact with
America was in a ruddy, eager-faced Army officer named
Dwight D. Eisenhower. These two had become good friends,
and far ahead lay an irony of a special kind: The Englishman
Macmillan (and a most unlikely politician he then appeared)
was eventually to follow Winston Churchill as the Queen's
first minister. The American Eisenhower, who had been se-
lected for spectacular promotion from a lieutenant-colonelcy
by Roosevelt on the recommendation of a general named
George C. Marshall, was to be the first professional military

man to reach the American Presidency since U. S. Grant—
and the first Republican to defeat a Democrat for President
since 1928. How much of all this had Roosevelt himself put
in train, this man who now lay dead while the bells tolled
and men and women wept in the nighttime? Who, or what,
"made" Eisenhower? FDR did in part. But so did chance and
circumstance.

Eisenhower had not the faintest idea of the new career that
lay in store for him as he dispatched from Supreme Head-
quarters, Allied Expeditionary Force in Europe his message
to Mrs. Roosevelt:

"The death of our great Commander in Chief comes as a
personal loss and grief to the millions of American fighting
men in this theater, who join me in extending to you our
heartfelt sympathy. We will continue and intensify our efforts
in order to insure that the great task which he undertook is
fulfilled in complete victory."

For Eisenhower, this day of Roosevelt's death would
remain forever a day not to be forgotten, as it would to
so many—mortar-platoon sergeants in actions scattered across
the world, hotel desk clerks in New York and Walla Walla,
Washington; little people, big people, middle people everywhere.

Macmillan, who was in the years ahead to meet Eisenhower
in many a conference designed to deal as best they both
could with the Soviet monolith that would rise so menacingly
after the war, had no special reason then to fix in his mind an
event of death so far away in Washington, D. C. His status
and his duty gave him other preoccupations.

Chapter

Four

But many others then of similarly useful if not greatly elevated stations still well recall the "12th April 1945," and will forever. One of these was a young lawyer named Adlai E. Stevenson, whose affairs were later to be most thoroughly mixed and mingled with those of an American political party. Stevenson, then an Assistant to the Secretary of State, was helping to prepare for the organizing conference of the United Nations at San Francisco. His boss in this work was Archibald MacLeish, who was an Assistant Secretary of State, and had already a gleam of that genius which was to establish him as one of the great poets and playwrights of our time.

Stevenson, as he recalls to me, was standing, idly, in MacLeish's big corner-room office in the old State, War and Navy Building in Washington, looking down into Seventeenth Street. The telephone rang. MacLeish listened and then said quietly to Stevenson, "The President is dead." It was MacLeish's immediate job to write the proclamation of death; Stevenson did what he could to help, by looking up precedents and so on.

MacLeish then produced what is by no measure the meanest work of his life. And it was one reflecting credit not alone on him but on the courage and wit and inventiveness—not to mention the devil-may-care—of a President who could bring so unlikely a fellow, a poet no less, into the heart of the bureaucracy itself. This was the proclamation, full of the aroma of the King James Bible and of the spirit of one of the true eggheads who served Roosevelt along with a good many self-nominated intellectuals who never quite earned that status:

"It has pleased God in His infinite wisdom to take from us the immortal spirit of Franklin Delano Roosevelt, the 32nd President of the United States.

"The leader of his people in a great war, he lived to see the assurance of the victory but not to share it. He lived to see the first foundations of the free and peaceful world to which his life was dedicated, but not to enter on that world himself.

"His fellow countrymen will sorely miss his fortitude and faith and courage in the time to come. The peoples of the earth who love the ways of freedom and of hope will mourn for him.

"But though his voice is silent, his courage is not spent, his faith is not extinguished. The courage of great men outlives them to become the courage of their people and the peoples of the world. It lives beyond them and upholds their purposes and brings their hopes to pass."

Stevenson's memory now is of "the shock and the hush of that spring evening." MacLeish the poet has much the same recall; but he speaks of it, of course, in a somewhat different way:

"I remember those hours very well. Somebody came in . . . to tell me FDR was dead. I remember his face working before he could say anything. I remember my saying No as if that disposed of it. Then they sent over from the White House to say that the [State] Department had to prepare the official announcement and that the Department meant me. I sent for Adlai who had an office next door and asked him to get somebody working on the precedents.

"Then for hours he and I batted drafts back and forth and finally I tore them all up and wrote whatever I wrote— I don't remember it at all and have never seen it since. By that time Adlai had, I think, gone, and I took the thing over to the White House and went home to Alexandria [Virginia]. It was after eight and Ada [Mrs. MacLeish] was in bed—she had gotten home late from a Red Cross trip and was dead tired. I remember kneeling beside her bed and sobbing. That was the first time. The next morning the Department had arranged to put me on the air and I started all right—talked for maybe five minutes—and then couldn't go on. That's what I remember. I think it's about right."

"Dead tired." So many were dead tired that evening and night—dead tired from so many years that had been bitter and demanding; dead tired from battles in the line overseas, from which men could still and would always remember the flat, smacking sound of the mortars, like heavy planks falling absolutely flat on a cement floor, the shrill cries of the little French children in the villages, "*Allemagne Kaput!*"; or dead tired from long trudging on that dreadfully dull, dreadfully gray, dreadfully crowded and often sordid thing called, with repellent cuteness, "the home front." Ada MacLeish at the Red Cross, Susie Jones at the USO, and all the Adas and the Susies everywhere for whom too much had happened too long and now too much had happened too quickly in the death of the man who had so long dominated so much of their lives.

While MacLeish was writing the nation's one formal and official farewell to Franklin D. Roosevelt, writing it from the point of view of one who had eagerly served the dead President, what of those who also had served him but had broken with him long before death brought an end to their quarrels?

Such a one was James A. Farley, the master politician who

had done much to bring Roosevelt from the Governor's Mansion at Albany to Washington. Farley, on that day, was in the Emerson Hotel in Baltimore, his lost dreams of the Vice-Presidency long since forgotten in the mind of a calmly realistic man who always had known how to accept defeat as well as victory.

"Big Jim" had gone to Baltimore to make a speech; and in his suite with him when the news came was Joseph Kearns of the Baltimore *News-Post*.

Farley's recollections now are, understandably, and quite properly, restrained:

"While I knew the President could not be in good health, judging by his appearance, I had no idea death was imminent. The news that he had passed on brought back memories of the years when I was closely associated with him, as Postmaster General and as Democratic State and National Chairman. I attended the funeral services in the White House and the burial services in Hyde Park."

"Judging by his appearance." This is an interesting, cool phrase, telling as it does of the rupture long before of one of the closest friendships in American politics. It is well to remember, though few, surely, could quite remember it on that day of death, that the great man who had gone was also a man quite capable of expending his friendship. The omelet cannot be made without breaking eggs; the Presidency cannot be run, by a strong and able man with a big heart but also with a hard, hard hand, without breaking hearts, even, sometimes, faithful hearts.

Among the obscurest of the obscure that day was another young man called Richard Nixon. Nixon, a lieutenant commander (Reserve) in the Navy was one of those uncounted thousands who held commissions-at-arms that had been signed, in theory anyhow, "Franklin D. Roosevelt." He had been rotated back to the States from the South Pacific and was currently stationed in Philadelphia with the less than stirring assignment of helping, as a lawyer, in the settlement of terminated war contracts.

He and Mrs. Nixon were having early dinner in a small restaurant in Philadelphia. A Negro waiter, tears in his eyes and slightly trembling, came to the table and told them, "Mr. Roosevelt is dead."

Nixon felt "shock and a void." But here, too, was a born politician, and so he felt something else as well. He was not then a very convinced Republican; in fact in the conscious sense politics was pretty well outside his life. But he needed no book or newspaper to tell him that a tremendous leader— and especially one with strange gifts to mobilize public opinion *anywhere*—had now died. And he wondered a great deal about what Mr. Truman would do with the Presidency.

There was another and even younger naval officer, a man named John Fitzgerald Kennedy, who—by fate, by accident, by whatever—was one day going to reach high place in this country but who, at the time, thought nothing of politics and very little of the man who had died in Warm Springs. A long time later—this was in 1960 while he was running for the Presidency of the United States—Kennedy told me in a brief and rather halting and somewhat wryly apologetic way, "I am afraid that at the time I had no deeply traumatic experience at all. I am afraid that my thoughts then came to this—and only this: that a powerful and colorful personality had passed." Kennedy did not mention a collateral circumstance that may perhaps have not encouraged in him, then, any long, historic, grand thoughts: He was on leave from the Navy, as a wounded officer, doing a bit of relaxing in a Miami, Florida, hospital.

It is extraordinary how the events and the emotions and the

circumstances of that day, of April 12, 1945, moved out in so vast a series of seemingly unrelated arcs and circles, to influence and even partly to determine the future as scattered wisps from a broken dream might, improbably, come to rest at last in foreordained patterns of reality. I have no warrant, from anything Nixon ever told me in so many words, to suppose for a moment that this day so long ago had any precisely measurable influence upon his own future life and career.

All the same, the fact is this: Upon Nixon at that hour in the little restaurant in Philadelphia—and indeed upon every man in either political party who would live to offer serious future challenge for the office Roosevelt had now put down in death—there descended from Roosevelt certain inescapable professional inheritance. No man after Shakespeare who ever wrote serious English was ever entirely free of Shakespeare's mastery of the language or ever wholly uninfluenced by that mastery, whether he knew it or not or wished it or not. So it was with Roosevelt. Many things he was to many men. And there was perhaps some truth, large or small, in all their infinitely varying views of him. But one thing he was, beyond the possibility of argument: He was, for his century at least, the master politician of what is politically the ablest race on this earth, the English-speaking race. And one thing he left beyond the possibility of argument. He left it impossible for any conceivable successor wholly to ignore his incredible technical skill as a politician—or wholly and absolutely to reject his incomparably brilliant techniques.

Lyndon Johnson, for an example, would find his place and stature as a mature politician because he had learned and grasped FDR's unrivaled power to win over nearly any other man in face-to-face relationships. Nixon would catch, or instinctively soak up, Roosevelt's special skill in first sensing, and then defining, and finally controlling and fully exploiting, the great, sometimes submerged issues which will move men with or even against their will. Rockefeller would discover how to turn wealth and position from handicaps into positive assets, as would John Kennedy. And so on, and on.

So April 12, 1945, was truly an extraordinary day. If it was the end of many things that had begun, it was also the beginning of some things that have not yet ended and may, indeed, never quite end. For the immeasurable political shadow that Roosevelt in life had cast upon our public affairs, and upon the public affairs of all the world, friendly and enemy alike, did not fade away with his breath in Warm Springs. The revolution that he had made had more to it than insuring bank deposits, establishing the old-age pension and remembering the forgotten man, though it had these too.

There are some who believe that the people, the masses, whatever term you will, are sometimes able to sense in certain critical hours in time the hushed movement of great and hidden fundamental forces which have no meaning or even existence to their conscious minds. I am one of those so believing. And I believe that the profound quiet of the crowd that night in Lafayette Square, and the profound quiet over much of this country and the world, had some such explanation. Ordinary tears there were, yes. Ordinary anxiety there was, yes. Questioning, of a vague and formless kind, there was, yes. But beyond all this was a kind of spiritual awareness, even among those who loved Roosevelt the most, of what could not be intellectually comprehended: that not only a man was gone, but a man who had stood, alone and with unique skill, at the core of a whole subtle complex of matters and things deeply touching and deeply conditioning every man's life. Would the complex now exist unaltered? Or had the man made and controlled the complex, rather than the complex made the man, so that what had been held in control and thus beneficent would be held in control no longer and thus malefic?

This question was the greatest of the many unknowns into which men and women stared into the blackening night of that black day in April. The blackest night was not, after all, in the consciousness of the death of this man of grandeur and of pettiness, of storied expertness and amazing naïveté, of rare power and rare weakness; this protector of whole peoples; this sword of the new social justice and this destroyer, sometimes, of the ancient justice; this gallant rescuer lightheartedly trampling upon good tradition as well as bad.

For it was for many, many things that people wept that night.

Chapter

Five

He had "lived to see the assurance of the victory but not to share it"—this was one of the phrases we read that night or the next morning and heard again and again on the radio. He had contributed second only to Churchill to the destruction of two sets of fascism across two oceans. The many who grieved that night—and the lesser number who openly or secretly exulted, in this country and elsewhere—knew that Roosevelt had led them across the seas and mountains and deserts to defeat Hitler and Tojo (and little Mussolini) and so to reclaim the most basic of all necessary assumptions, the assumption that in this life some elementary decencies *must* be maintained. The loftiest monument that history could possibly raise to Franklin Delano Roosevelt was simply to the fact that he cared, and finally showed that he cared, when the anguished cries of the brutalized and the terrorized so rose across the Atlantic as to force their way into the consciousness of every man whose heart was not made altogether of stone. Roosevelt would not forever shut his ears to this long, this rising, this hopeless moan. For he knew that it rose not alone from the Jewish and Polish and other victims of the Nazis but also from the soul of mankind.

He had not, however, moved instantly or with instant gallantry. Hitler had given seven years of mountingly ghastly evidence of what he was about before Franklin Roosevelt began to take the first hesitant steps toward meeting this unexampled challenge to man's humanity. The 1940 campaign had been notable for his promises "again and again" that the sons of this country would not be sent to fight "in foreign wars." This was, of course, a pledge of highly debatable integrity; it was, in plain fact, a false promise. No informed and compassionate person in this country in the autumn of 1940 doubted that Hitler's defeat must be brought about and that an American participation to this end was inevitable. (Some, of whom I was surely one, thought, too, that it was morally unavoidable, inevitable or not.)

All the same, the leader in the White House had approached our involvement with great hesitation and without relish. If one had asked of the crowd in Lafayette Square, on that night of death, what the dead man had been, the common reply from a hundred throats would have been this: "A great internationalist." The crowd had been caught up—and to this day the crowd remains caught up—in a curious error: Roosevelt was not at his death, and never was, essentially an internationalist. Basically and at heart he was a nationalist, full of the first and universal quality of American nationalists, which is fear and suspicion of Britain and of alliances. It had been long since forgotten by the evening of April 12, 1945, that Franklin Roosevelt's first foreign policy action in his long tenure was to destroy the London Economic Conference. His heart, until the unexampled world convulsions brought about by Hitler simply forced a change of interest, was always in domestic affairs, and homely domestic affairs, at that. Conservationism lay in him as the deepest of all motives, as he had shown in long concern for the wasted forests and eroded plains far antedating his arrival in the White House, and as he had shown a hundred times when, early in his administration, he was grappling with the central problem of conserving the capitalistic economy of *this* country and conserving its human resources, its men and women and children.

Roosevelt himself, at least, knew what he was.

Among the countless Roosevelt papers in the memorial library in Hyde Park, New York, is a memorandum from FDR to his press secretary, Stephen Early, which made with chilling vigor these points:

That Roosevelt himself had never felt American interests and those of Western Europe to be necessarily, or even usually, the same.

That he regarded as "pure invention" talk that his whole upbringing had been internationalist in tone.

That he had never in his life forgotten that "the Roosevelt family in the West Indian sugar business was compelled to contend many years against the British and French interests in those Islands—and that is what made them revolutionaries rather than Tories in 1776."

That the Delano family—FDR's mother's side—had historically fought the British as bitter competitors in the old China trade. "I [FDR] was brought up on the story of how the Delano family's principal competitors were the British. . . . Warren Delano [the President's grandfather] was the United States agent in China during the whole [American] Civil War and spent most of his time fighting against the British interests which, at that time, were wholly on the side of the Confederacy."

That FDR did not know England as a boy but did know Germany and "if anything I looked upon the Germany I knew with far more friendliness than I did on Great Britain or France."

The notion that he was a born interventionist in world affairs, an eager reformer of the globe, could not have been more incorrect—or more widely held. The very human conditions of his own life made him at bottom a parochial man (if parochialism may be stretched to encompass the affairs of a nation). He was a squirearch, a man born to look after the *home* place, and never an "aristocrat," though that appellation was endlessly assigned to him.

The people may hold the aristocrat in high regard and respect and even awe. And when he dies they may feel that a chill, majestic change has come over their affairs. But the people rarely weep for aristocrats. When they wept that night for Franklin Roosevelt their instinct told them what their minds did not. The man who had departed was neither of aristocratic lineage nor of aristocratic motivations; his heritage was sturdily upper-middle-class, his motivations, as to the war, were closely enough akin to their own to be instantly understandable to them and never alien to them.

Their senses knew, if their minds did not formulate the thought (those, that is, who did not oppose automatically each and every thing he stood for and did), that he had avoided the climactic test of war as long as he could and as prudently as he could. They never supposed—and they were quite right—that he had taken this great and reluctant country into the maelstrom for any of the outmoded reasons of the aristocrat: for *noblesse oblige*, to make the *beau geste*, to lose all for glory and honor, to die in the gallantly lively company of one's peers. He had made a great war record, but mainly because it happened that as head of so rich and powerful a country he had so much in mass of matériel and men to throw into the struggle once events and his own slowly formed inclinations brought him into it.

The people of this country did not know it that night, or yet for many nights to come, but the plain truth was this: The President who had shown such incomparable skill in the affairs of this country alone and had so greatly helped to win a world war had profoundly compromised the winning of any possible subsequent peace. This was one of the supreme legacies he left. (I say this as one who admired and loved him, and still do, and as one who resented and still resents the petty and savage nature of some of his opposition. You can, if you are grown up, reckon that a man was great without supposing him to be without large and even terrible flaws, including flaws which well may haunt his world for generations after he is gone. And you will realize, if you are grown up, that the capacity for stubborn and brilliant direction and mastery of other men carries within it, invariably, the capacity for monumental error and massive mischief.)

For the American squirearch over and over again, through the superior force that he led and represented, had been able unwisely to overcome the wartime comrade he both liked and disliked (and distrusted), Winston Churchill. Of this pair it was the aristocratic Churchill (who despised, for example, the homely housing programs and the like which always enchanted FDR) who had the correct view of the nature of the struggle and the incredible difficulties that would follow when that struggle had at length been won. Not all the qualities of the aristocracy are attractive or useful. But there is one aristocratic quality which is indispensable in all truly vast designs. It was one which Churchill had abundantly and Roosevelt never had at all. This is the quality of an almost disdainful private detachment; a long, long, ancestral memory that rejects both too much love and too much hate; a willingness to die quietly, if need be, but never to be caught out in a sentimentalism or a cliché of thought. It is, in short, a deeply worldly quality, a profound sophistication, an informed cynicism, in the face of which Roosevelt was hardly more than a still young and eager, if incomparably powerful, man from Groton and Harvard and the Upper Hudson.

Roosevelt, once his country was in a war which old Churchill had long been fighting alone while with grand, aristocratically candid maneuvers he slowly drew his natural ally here to his side, set out to justify the association with Bolshevik Russia now entailed. He suggested that there really was freedom of a sort in Russia. Churchill, for his part, stood in Commons and answered the taunts of his minuscule Communist and pro-Communist bloc of baiters with the haughty frankness of his class. Yes, he *had* said long ago that Bolshevism should have been strangled at birth. He did not now take it back; not a syllable of it. But he would say this: He, Winston Churchill, would gladly make a pact with the Devil if the Devil would assist him in killing Germans.

This difference in the two great leaders was immensely significant. For Roosevelt had fought the war and helped plan the postwar world with mixed equipment. There was a lively —and critically useful—determination to win it, militarily. There was an almost mechanical suspicion of perfidious Albion—though, by the richest of irony, he himself was endlessly accused, by anti-Rooseveltians at home, of being a sort of stooge of Albion. There was an unsleeping antagonism to "colonialism," of which Britain was of course the copyright holder.

This was a curiously revealing thing: Anticolonialism was the byword and hallmark of American isolationists and near-isolationist American nationalists long before the liberals took it up as a rallying cry. Never troubling FDR, or even seriously engaging his attention, was the manifest fact that semicolonial, colonial and imperial positions, from Iceland to the far Pacific, formed the sole means and bases permitting the Allies at last to go on the counteroffensive and so to win the war. The British Isles themselves, the very home of both imperialism and colonialism, stood at the forefront of these positions.

And there was in FDR a fixed notion, never acknowledged in so many words but manifest again and again in his dealings with his allies, that only he really understood Stalin, that only he could really deal with Stalin, and that only he really had nothing to fear from Stalin. This estimate, though terribly wrong, was in many ways understandable—if more understandable at the time than now in hindsight. In the first place, it should never for a moment be forgotten that the profession of politics is an art not merely of compromise but of a peculiar—what might be called an impersonal and inherent —cruelty. And Roosevelt was a supreme, a born, practitioner of the art of politics. Great politicians no less than small ones see power as the very first reality, power even ahead of the desire ably and disinterestedly to serve, for one cannot do the one without having the other.

Roosevelt loved power not only for his own sake but also for its own sake. And because he put power at so lofty a place in his own hierarchy of values there was a tinge of an in-evitable—and also friendly—contempt in his view toward as-sociates, who, no matter the grandeur of their stature, were short of this essential quality. To put the thing crudely but with complete truthfulness, Churchill had come to the alliance in the first place with hat in hand. This Roosevelt never for-got; nor did he ever allow Churchill quite to forget it.

Was this dead man Roosevelt, then, not actually a monster of a sort? Should his people not have withheld their tears after all, on this night of death? Of course he was not; and of course they should not. Expressive of all that he was were all the qualities that made him what he was. I am a professional political writer of long experience, if nothing else, and very wide acquaintance among the practitioners of the art. And I never knew a truly able politician, liberal or conservative, Republican or Democrat, Northerner or Southerner, who was not deeply vain (if justifiably so) underneath—and quite tough enough, underneath, to cut down his own brother if that brother should become objectively expendable to objec-tively higher demands.

Then, there was this subtle, but important, fact: Roosevelt, though never for a moment concerned in the fine-spun and rather archly niggling ideologies of the American Left or Right, was nevertheless a consciously "modern" man in politics. Actually, I think, he looked at Churchill, an old politician and a Tory one at that, rather as he looked at American conservative and traditionalist politicians such as old Senator Walter George of Georgia. He was fond of them; but he saw them really, as genteel anachronisms, valuable personal relics to be treasured, but relics all the same of a time that had gone.

Clemenceau of France, a generation before, had thought war too important to be left to the generals. Roosevelt had thought it too important to be left to the Churchills.

Then, too, in the late Thirties the atmosphere of the United States had been soaked with a reformist political view which was as right and useful in our domestic affairs as it was foolish and inopportune in our foreign and allied affairs. The general tone of the "best minds"—and in plain fact they *were*, on the whole, the best minds—demanded a liberalism of welfarism at home and supported abroad the concept of the Popular Front against fascism. Howling partisan extremists, usually Republicans but sometimes center-to-right Democrats as well, saw this as a "Communist" movement. The charge, as to Roosevelt himself, as to his Administration and as to the vast majority of the suspected intellectuals, was the silliest of rubbish. Roosevelt was about as much a "Communist" as was the Pope; the truth is that he was unbearably bored, as good Anglo-American politicians have always been, by all dogmatic and schematic views of politics. He simply believed in pragmatism, as did the thoroughly pragmatic politician Truman, who now moved wonderingly about his new home in the White House. Roosevelt only made use of the doctrinaires, in such ways and at such times as he felt them useful.

Chapter

Six

Still, the country's whole intellectual aura—which Roosevelt had helped to create by bringing "the professors" into government in their eager academic swarms—had had meaning, even to him. It was not at all pro-Communist. In the deepest sense it was only profoundly antifascist. But in a lesser but still significant sense it was something more as well. It was also anti-Tory and antitraditionalist, in part because some Tories and some traditionalists had been all too tolerant of fascism itself. Churchill, even to Roosevelt, not only was a man of the past, but he also was in the wrong intellectual club, even though he had been the West's lonely sentinel against Hitlerism for years before the New Liberals had taken up the cause in any important way.

Roosevelt, moreover, had approached the war's problems in the notion, fully justified by his domestic experience, that slogans, high-minded and quite sincere ones, could themselves become the partial solvents of great issues and mighty contests at arms. (It might be recalled here in passing that a certain subsequent Administration, headed by a Roosevelt general named Dwight D. Eisenhower, was not in fact actually to invent sloganeering as a policy in itself.) To nearly every wartime conference with Churchill, FDR had carried some new proposed manifesto—the four freedoms and unconditional surrender among them—just as he had carried the suggestions of associates like Henry Morgenthau, Jr., for a *public* declaration that we would certainly not let the Germans off lightly after it was all over.

Churchill's whole instinct had been to resist all this. He knew that the four freedoms, so lightheartedly and so honorably promised, would not in fact be obtainable—as both he and Roosevelt must make all too clear in the treatment of so tragic a war victim as Poland, whose prostrate body was largely to be handed over to the Russians. He knew, too, that by the literal German mind unconditional surrender would be read to mean what the Germans would surely have meant had the shoe been on the other foot. (Many a man, including this writer, can testify that the doctrine of unconditional surrender caused the Germans to fight harder; I, for one, remember SS officers firing their pistols into our people in Normandy from the very ground on which they lay as prisoners.) "Think of it always; speak of it never." This was the unsuccessful Churchill view of how to plan the matter of revenge and justice once the war had been won. And he knew, too, what would and did come about: We, who had been so insistent upon warning the Germans in advance of their fate, would be less firm than the British when the time came to exact payment.

Thus it was that the President lying dead on that April night had left us more bereft in some ways than we knew.

The United States of America had been flung by destiny into a role for which it was unready and for which its late President, in some ways the ablest leader it had known in all its history, had been most peculiarly unready, and unfitted. Already on that night of April 12, 1945, some of the bitter-end opposition were, as Rayburn had foreseen, indeed making ready to dance all over the grave not yet dug. The dance these opponents were rehearsing was an ugly thing, a grotesque ballet of misrepresentation and oversimplification, a pantomime of animus which would present the dead President as a warmonger who had tricked the Japanese into attacking us at Pearl Harbor and had consciously made the world safer for Communism.

"They" were making ready to slander the motives and the purposes, and the actions as well, not merely of a President who had fallen, but of a country—their own country—which had risen to provide the climactic power for the most noble crusade against massive evil that the world had known.

It could have been said with some truth—and on that night it was fiercely muttered by many through their tears and their slowly spent sorrow as a *total* truth—that Franklin Roosevelt lay dead as much from the malice of his enemies at home as from the limitless exertions of his mind and body and heart in his long struggle to overcome the country's enemies from without.

This, however, was not really the whole truth, nor yet the truth unalloyed. What the President had done was this: He had taken one really wise decision of grand strategy, and only one. Over and over through the war's course he had again shown his mastery of the home scene by compelling his countrymen to take and keep the sound course of selecting the Germans rather than the Japanese as the first and the real enemy in the contest. This had been no small accomplishment, for the unexampled brutality of the shock at Pearl Harbor had set a raging fever running through this country. And its people would surely have preferred to fling their whole weight and their military cutting edge into the Pacific war. Roosevelt himself surely would have preferred, had reality given him the option, to do the same.

For he was a blue-water President, a big-Navy President, something of an old salt himself, if a civilian one. His first national service had been as Assistant Secretary of the Navy back in Woodrow Wilson's Administration. He was not, remotely, an Army type; either as a person or as a politician.

And this was not the least of the great shortcomings of FDR as a war President. He was sentimentally a part of a tradition of an outmoded naval romanticism which, splendidly defiant of the facts of life of modern warfare, was apt unwisely to shape his thinking whenever and wherever his conscious mind was not specially on gaurd.

The Navy types had tended to think of the war in Europe as messily "political"—as, God knows, it was—and not nearly so much our business as was the war against the infernally presumptuous Japanese. Their notion, generally, was not to get mixed up with all those British and French and other foreigners on the Continent but rather to send the grand fleets grandly steaming out to teach the Japanese a good lesson. They were essentially isolationist, notwithstanding the fact that their whole past careers had been, in the purely geographic sense, far more international than had those of the Army types. They had never understood that war was no longer professional and final in its results; that it was, instead, genuinely global, resting upon an almost measureless mass of amateur fighters whose principal function had to be the literal clearing of the earth's terrain of fascist power and whose highest hope could be a merely tolerable, and never a final, military solution *possibly* leading to endurable subsequent political solutions. War, in short, was no longer for the warriors. It was a supreme, a convulsive but also sustained effort in concert of all that this and other nations had and were. It was no longer a contest of thrust and parry among elite forces; it had to be the glacierlike movement of the *sum total of all the power, of every kind and context,* that the free world would counterpose against the vast, glacierlike entrenchments of fascism. Thus its highest requirements were mass and men; its harsh realities made the basic mission of Navy not so much one of fighting but really rather one of carrying things, or safeguarding the carrying of things. The

greatest single naval victory of the war was the slowly
achieved ability to deliver the goods across the Atlantic; it
was an epic not of offense but of defense; a saga not so much
of derring-do but simply of holding on. It was the protection of Allied *mass*. The Army mind understood mass—mass
such as would be required to win the partial military victory
in prospect, and mass such as would be the first requirement
to avert the physical vacuums of chaos which the cease-fire
would bring in many lands.

Roosevelt, to his credit, especially considering his own emotional pro-Navy indoctrination, to a point had held off the
Navy type, not to mention a significant part of a largely Middle Western public opinion which, because of the ties of old
Germanic blood, was much less ready to go after the Germans
than it ought to have been. To make and sustain the policy
of "Europe first" had involved, moreover, complications of
other human kinds. One of these complications had resulted
in lifting a lieutenant colonel called Eisenhower from ob-
scurity to world position.

The best wartime military mind in the United States was
that of an old aide to General John J. Pershing named George
Catlett Marshall.

That this was also the most coolly unselfish mind in high
place in the United States was fortuitous or—as I prefer to
put it—providential. Marshall, as Army Chief of Staff, had been
by all logic the obvious, the inevitable choice for Supreme
Allied Commander in Europe once we had entered the war
and the European theater had been given priority. Indeed, the
British had long assumed that it would be Marshall—and Marshall it would have been but for the great difficulties raised
here at home by the right doctrine of Europe First.

FDR had toyed with the idea of sending Marshall to Europe
anyhow, but the decision had at length been reached that this
could not be done without tearing the thin fabric of national

unity which gave at best only tolerable acceptance to Europe First. General Marshall, it was decided, was indispensable at home. Marshall himself would go to his grave refusing to voice so much as a murmur of private disappointment that the dull work had been left to him and the glamour to the much junior Dwight Eisenhower. I myself, who had the great honor to know Marshall well, asked him many times to tell me how he felt about it all; always he only looked glacially at me and changed the subject.

All the same, in making Marshall the top American war lord subordinate only to his own quite humanly adequate vanity as the supremest of all the field marshals, FDR had still clung to his overriding faith in the Navy. He had made Fleet Admiral William D. Leahy his personal Chief of Staff. (Marshall told me once that he was delighted with this appointment—first because FDR had chosen a naval officer, and second because the President had granted, actually at Marshall's suggestion, a rank for Leahy higher than Marshall's own. "The Navy," George Marshall said with a thin smile, "wanted place and position and perquisite; I was most happy for them to have it and so get them off *my* back. I had to run the war, and I wanted, naturally, to do it with as few unnecessary distractions as possible.")

Nevertheless, Leahy and Admiral Ernest J. King, the Chief of Naval Operations, had offered many distractions. They tended always to influence FDR's war thinking toward parochialism and toward a certain anachronistic view of the struggle. They had kept alive all his suspicions of the British; they had much reinforced his own instinctive notions that "Dr. Win-the-War," as FDR called his successor policy to that of "Dr. New Deal," was the only thing that really mattered.

But the trouble was that FDR's policy of Dr. Win-the-War had been appallingly oversimplified. He had believed always, as was made very clear later in dozens of memoirs, that he understood winning the peace quite as well as he understood winning the war. Over and over, he had pressed upon Churchill a sunny view made up of two equally dangerous assumptions: that he, Roosevelt, could easily handle Josef Stalin; and that Stalin anyhow was a well-meaning old chap who would not give the world much trouble once Hitler had been destroyed.

No one in this country knew it, then, but precisely one hour before Roosevelt died that day in Warm Springs he had sent a note to Churchill urging—indeed instructing—the old Briton to "minimize the general Soviet problem as much as possible." For, Roosevelt went on to Churchill, "most of them [Soviet problems] always straighten out." The German collapse was fast proceeding then; and it was at this point that Roosevelt's notions had left to us perhaps the gravest and the most nearly insoluble danger ever thrown down before the American people: Churchill had wanted the armies of the West to remain in some parts of the Soviet Zone in Germany until the West had firm agreements with the Russians as to the fate of Central Europe—not to say of Berlin itself. Harry Truman, who had so abruptly been thrust into a job for which his dead predecessor had given him little information and less preparation, was stuck with the arrangements Roosevelt had made about Germany, and about other things. Churchill would sent to Truman a cable expressing his profound misgivings at the withdrawal of American forces "to our line of occupation in the central sector of Germany, thus bringing Soviet power into the heart of Western Europe and the descent of an iron curtain between us and everything to the Eastward.

"Nothing really important has been settled yet [with the Russians] and you and I will have to bear great responsibility for the future," the Prime Minister would go on. Truman would reply to this in the only way he could reply; he simply would say that the United States could not repudiate Roosevelt's promise to occupy only certain areas of Germany.

All this was in the foreground of a tragic backdrop already created by FDR in his long and successful insistence upon putting nearly the whole of the Allied invasion effort directly across the English Channel against Germany. Churchill and his military people had argued endlessly and in vain for major invasion efforts in Southern Europe as well so as to throw a line of Western force across Stalin's then private purpose to move massively into Eastern Europe—and never to draw out again.

Thus the worn man now dead had fought his war all to well but his peace all too poorly. He had left his countrymen without his incomparable domestic leadership; he had left them also with a new world almost as menacing in its way, from the Russians in the East, as it had recently been from the Germans in Central Europe. What all this would open out for the future was an all but indescribable clutch of harsh and bitter problems. The man now President of the United States and sitting alone that night in the old mansion at 1600 Pennsylvania Avenue in Washington knew almost literally nothing of what had gone before in our high policies and of what was even then in preparation in our grand military policies. Truman had been a member of the Senate but he had not been one of those who stood on the inside there; and so he did not even know at first that Roosevelt had put billions into something so secret that only few were put abreast of the work. This was the development of the atomic bomb, the weapon that was to bring in a new age of mankind, an age no less fundamental in meaning than the age that brought the use of iron. Truman knew very little about the Yalta Conference, for example—this conference which was to open Roosevelt's memory and the whole body of the Democratic

Party to powerful and successful domestic attack for years to come. He knew so little, indeed, that when James F. Byrnes, who was then Secretary of State, would first mention it to him, Truman would humbly ask this subordinate if he would be so kind as to *provide the President of the United States with a stenographic report of what had gone on there.*

Curiously, however, the man who was universally supposed to be only a small and parochial domestic politician would within a week exhibit to those inside the Administration a quality almost of grandeur. Certainly, too, he would show instinctive skill in dealing with the vast foreign matters to which he had been so total a stranger.

For before that April was out Harry Truman would have taken the measure of the toughest Foreign Minister the Bolsheviks ever had, the glacial Molotov. On April 13, before he had been a day in his new office, Truman would be aware that Stalin was not living up to the Yalta agreements. He would send a message to Churchill showing this awareness. He called Molotov to the White House and in his Missouri way he examined that opaque-faced Russian closely about Soviet intentions. He told Molotov flatly he was far from satisfied with what the Soviet Union was doing and added to him that there was not going to be any one-way street in international cooperation. Molotov, professing himself deeply hurt, replied: "I have never been talked to like that in my life." Mr. Truman, who never had any pacifist inclinations, retorted with nasal calm: "Carry out your agreements and you won't get talked to like that." This is the way Truman described the conversation in his *Memoirs.* But I don't think I am mistaken in my recollection that on one occasion in talking to me his report of what he really told Molotov was far saltier than it was in his book.

Chapter

Seven

At all events here was the new President—a man who never
would have dreamed of aspiring to the job—left in this position: He had to liquidate a war in which he had had almost
no part. He had to take on an enormous burden as chief
sponsor of what was then only a prospect, the United Nations. He had to dig about frantically, in the White House
records, in the State Department records, and among friends
and associates in the government itself, to find out where we
had already been and to what we had already been committed. Hardly less moving that night than the great fact
that Franklin Roosevelt was dead was the then totally un-
considered fact that the living Truman had suddenly accepted
a burden of a kind never before thrust so heavily and so soon
upon any public man in the world. Nevertheless the change
of Administrations—no, more than that, the leap from one
whole era into another—would proceed with a kind of inevitable stability. It would be perhaps the finest vindication
for our system that had been recorded since the War Between the States had ended the greatest previous peril to
Constitutional government in this country.

". . . the first foundations of the free and peaceful world
to which his life was dedicated."

These "foundations" were in fact very thin. They were
built not even on sand but only upon hope and accident

(Roosevelt's death) and the crazy fortuities of the system that, all the same, was somehow going to muddle through. The climactic hours of the life of the great man now lying dead had been spent in work for which his genius was ill-met. He had been forced to halt a work of unexampled skill in restoring and increasing the inner strength and decency of his own country. But for the task of bringing to the world a fruitful peace after a wasting war he had been sadly inadequate.

Roosevelt had made The Bomb. But circumstances had left it to Truman to decide whether The Bomb should be dropped and so to open, if then only in prospect, an armaments race of so perilous a kind as to make the Nobels, the Krupps, the Vickers group and their like seem in retrospect to have been mere children playing with firecrackers and sparklers. There is no reason to reckon that FDR would have made a decision any different from that which Truman would later make, which was to loose the fury upon the Japanese at Nagasaki and Hiroshima. Given the massive weight of the estimates of Secretary of War Henry L. Stimson and others that to storm the Japanese home islands might cost half a million military casualties, who could suppose that Roosevelt would have said No to the use of this then "ultimate weapon"? But there is still this: This most terrible politico-moral judgment of all time, a judgment dwarfing any heretofore made by any President, or king or dictator, had yet to be made when FDR passed from life to death. The Large Man was spared its agony. The supposedly Small Man, in one of the most exquisite of the paradoxes which most of all govern all life, would alone have to face it; to face history and all the unknowable future from this moment of lonely decision. (I have suggested before this that the moment of death was a total parting, a breakage, in the rope of time itself; I should be willing, if there were need for it, to rest the case for that opinion on this circumstance alone.)

On that April night of farewell to FDR, even more than this transcendental turn—this turn from an era where world war was possible to an era where world war was unspeakable and inconceivable—was on foot. For whatever reason, fate or chance, the Small Man would be here to do the work that the Large Man had not well done.

The change would come, as does nearly all important and deep change, in many ways, discernible and indiscernible. All over our public affairs it would move, sometimes unnoticed and many times not even faintly understood. Perhaps it was just because Harry Truman had been an artillery captain in the First World War and still, indeed, wore his overseas cap and marched in the American Legion's parades. (I think not; but have it this way, if you will.) At all events, within weeks under Truman the controlling mind of military policy was to pass, under his direction, from what had been largely the dominance (but for Marshall) of Navy and Air. Navy's view of the war then ending had been parochial, anachronistic and largely irrelevant to reality but for the Pacific theater, which had been magnificently and with gallantry cleared by Navy in what was the last series of essentially nineteenth-century battles to mark the twentieth century—and the last, surely, the world was ever to know. Air's view toward the war that was closing (and toward any war that might lie in the distance) was quite simple: Destroy enough enemy cities, kill enough enemy people (civilian or combat), and there you are. Navy never believed that war was a part of politics; Air's situation was even simpler—Air did not believe in politics itself.

Army, however, which had always been the humblest and least demanding of the three services and had done nine tenths of the dying in the Second World War, knew that war was politics, international politics, of course. And so would Truman, the Small Man who was in simple fact to become much bigger than the Large Man in big things. (Sam Rayburn once told me, from all the remembered experience of nearly fifty years of high place in Washington, that the least partisan President he ever knew in foreign affairs—and one of the most partisan in home affairs—was Harry S. Truman. This remark consciously included both Roosevelt and Woodrow Wilson. Only weeks after Truman had come to office in succession to Roosevelt he would have the Congressional leaders down to the White House to discuss a grand foreign-policy plan, the Truman Doctrine for the postwar salvation of Greece and Turkey from imperialist Communism. Truman would outline what he proposed to do and would ask for comment. One of the Congressional deputation would ask, "But what, Mr. President, what of the political implications to the party of all this?" Truman would turn in cold anger upon him and say slowly, "In *these matters* I never want to hear that damn word politics mentioned here again.")

Truman's Army view—and it was frankly this, for Truman never hid his great debt to Marshall and others from the Army—would be in no way so simple as Navy's or Air's. Army already had the task of beginning the occupation period in Germany and Japan; of feeding as well as policing. The Army-Truman mind already had the task of outrunning chaos in the conquered lands by relief and rehabilitation, while Truman personally had to help set the United Nations agoing. The Marshall Plan would be made, to set Europe on its feet again.

Truman would at once put his eye on Marshall, who was to become, with Truman's own full acceptance, much of the intellect and heart (if a well-contained and cool heart) of the successor Administration, first as Secretary of State and then as Secretary of Defense. If one wanted to speak in cheap alliteration it might be said that the Humility of Harry would be the first and most recurrent note in the new White House medley.

For the Large Man upon whose death most of us brooded that night had been, in a way, too *personally* large to deal properly with what now had to be done; too *personally* large to bring out from those, like Marshall, who were now needed to save us, the full qualities now so much required. It was not merely that in Warm Springs that day the life of a President had come to a sudden end; it was also that the institution of the Presidency had been returned, in the space of a single failing heartbeat, from the personal to the collective. One could not have imagined Marshall's being able to perform for Roosevelt as he was to do with Truman; there was too much of the Anglo-Dutch patroon in the one and too much of the disciplined obedience of a lifetime in the other. The second member of the Marshall-Acheson pair who was to loom so large so long in our affairs, Dean Acheson, had himself rather proved the point. He had not been able long to bear Roosevelt, or Roosevelt had not been able long to bear him, in the Roosevelt Administration.

So, we were turning that night (though we did not know it) not merely from a phase of war to a phase of a peace (of sorts) and not merely from one Administration to another. We were turning also from the period of the Great Leader, singular, to a period of a more generalized leadership, plural. This new leadership was to confront problems actually far more complex than the war itself had presented. The contrast actually was to be more marked even than that, say, from Theodore Roosevelt on San Juan Hill to Woodrow Wilson in Paris talking of a League of Nations just after the First

World War. Franklin Roosevelt was to be the last great *personal* President. And now, there were to be no more parades; but instead only a long, gray time in which we should prosper mightily in goods and wage rates and profits and living standards while we lived in a quiet, universal fear of an abiding new kind of war, a cold war infinitely more sophisticated than the hot war which Roosevelt had so helped to win.

Economic depression would very shortly become only a series of terrible memories of the middle-aged. The rusting railroad lines of the Depression, the drab boxcars from which shivering men crawled lifelessly in the endless rainy, chill autumn dawns of those days, the soup kitchens, the apple merchants, the bleak suicides of ruined financiers, large and small, the unsleeping sense of guilt among those of us who were lucky enough to go on being employed and paid while our brothers lived in a hopeless deprivation which this new country of limitless opportunity had never before known —this long, searing, traumatic nightmare would be over for good and all. *This* war FDR *had* really won; to many millions he was and would forever remain the shepherd who had truly cared for the flock. And this feeling was right and good. For it is not yet possible to say that the enemy—want—that he had soundly and permanently defeated here at home was any less evil, though it was surely less measurably destructive, than the foreign enemy far less soundly and far less surely laid low. The man who has clothed and fed others may be more grieved for by the people when he goes than the man who may have saved for them something that can only be called, vaguely, a system or a way of life.

To know hunger for one's self and one's family and not to find food; to see despair in them and not to be able to find hope for them; to know how to work and not to be able to find work to do for them—all this is worse than death itself. Any good man can face death in action, not happily, but at least manfully. But few men, good or bad, can face the incurable, the desperate wound to soul itself of that state of affairs in which man must at last acknowledge that he cannot care for even those to whom most of all he owes care.

So, in the first hours of a ragged, unorchestrated and ill-formed national symphony of elegy that night there was only one absolutely clear theme. The theme was farewell to the good squire. What he had done for his people at home, to protect their right to bread and work and shelter, would live for decades, certainly, and perhaps forever. This strong structure of economic security had been marvelously built, built to endure, and the people somehow knew this.

But the incomparable armies that Roosevelt had raised (no less than the great hopes he had raised for a postwar world) were at this very hour of his death about to become obsolete. Very soon the Johnny who had got his gun was to be shuffling along in that great retreat which we were to call "bringing the boys home."

And Harry Truman would soon proclaim V-J Day from the White House, and so the end of it all. The mightiest war machine ever brought together by one nation (it was much better, then, than all that the Soviets had, though this is not easy to remember now) had little further use in it. It was to be Truman who was actually to preside over a dismantlement of a force that would inextricably involve, as well, the progressive liquidation of the Western Free World position all over Eastern and Central Europe but for the terribly exposed pockets of Berlin and West Germany.

If one could have known that night what was to become

so clear in the afterlight, his tears for a truly great man who had died would have been none the fewer and none the less real.

But there would have been other tears, too—of grief for the tragic inheritance left by that man at the end of a victory gallantly won, militarily, and tragically compromised for the future. The King had died and the captains were departing, to retirement or advancement in the new world now opening. The war that some of the captains (Eisenhower and Montgomery, notably) had called a crusade had been a crusade in truth, in its destruction of the fungus of fascism. But this night of the shuttered lights in the White House was a night not only of elegy for a man; it was an hour also of recessional for a nation. No leader can wholly control the future, and no leader can properly be held to account for not managing to hold back such tides of history as may be beyond man's reckoning or staying hand. But this man who had so nobly done so much *for* us had also, in his pride and stubbornness, done *to* us what he never intended. He had closed the past by opening for us an unknowable future which, as it unfolded with slow inevitability, was to remove the locus of world power from the West toward the East for the first time since the first Crusades of so many dusty centuries before.

Chapter

Eight

Never before this night had we said farewell so poignantly to so much. Farewell to a man loved by massive millions, disliked and distrusted by fewer millions, ardently and acridly hated by hundreds of thousands—though very powerful hundreds of thousands they were. Farewell to a past which for all its vast complications was still less complex than the future then beginning for us in the tolling of the many bells. Farewell to the mixed memories of twelve years of a nation first paralyzed and then freed in farm and shop and market place; of a nation first softly unprepared for war, then carried along gingerly toward that war, then triumphantly, if belatedly, armed so amply and so decisively. Farewell (for many reasons, most of them going back to Roosevelt's faults but some of them to arise from Truman's mistakes) to that brief hour in which we, the United States of America, had stood, hardly knowing it, at the pinnacle of world power as we never had stood before—and as, perhaps, we were never, never to stand again.

Goodbye . . . Goodbye . . . Goodbye—this single word, surely, was in our minds, if not always on our lips, as it had not ever been before at the hour of the death of an American leader. The feeling was something like that rising in the aching throats of men on a troopship as it lifts anchor from familiar port and steams out, in fog and blackout, with never a band

playing and never so much as a single, dying, answering farewell from the shore. Yes, it was like this, in that one felt a
nostalgia—for he knew not quite what. But it was much more
than this. For it was farewell not simply to the large, grand
things like the war and the world power we had lately won
and already lost. It was farewell also to some dull, homely
things, one of which was to a whole political era at home.

The Roosevelt Revolution, as so many had called it, had
died, too, in Warm Springs. And just as his great armies were
now shortly to be broken up on many foreign fronts, so the
extraordinary domestic political army of the Roosevelt New
Deal was now to be dispersed at home. The armies sent abroad
had first been jumped-up, ill-equipped affairs, back here in
the training areas. (Remember the wooden guns with which
some of us early infantry types were initially "trained" in the
swampy Camps Cornpone of the South and the bleak and
blowing Camps This and That of the North?) But these
armies, well-weaponed later on and -blooded from North Af-
rica to the Elbe to Iwo Jima, had come more than into their
own, long before the great show was over everywhere.

Such had been the history of the Army of the New Deal
which FDR had raised at home. By acute instinct, by stretching and patching, by putting round pegs into square holes
and mixing up Brain Trusters with semiliterate shoeshine boys
and aristocratic Delta planters with Pittsburgh steel workers
he had set off to raise this army of Democrats and more-or-less
Democrats, and old-time Populists, and tired Socialists and
recanting Republicans.

At first, back in the early Thirties, it had been, in political
terms, another of those Camp Cornpone outfits. It had been
led with a gay and deceptive seeming recklessness by a man
in the White House who had tilted an impudently long ciga-

rette holder upward at fate; who had cried out his compassion for "the forgotten man" in an unforgotten broad *a* which, for all his ability at demagoguery when demagoguery had been needed, he had never sought to alter into more "American" diction. In the years since, this new political party, still called the Democratic Party but also a far larger thing than that, had been marshaled and hectored and everbroadened by this extraordinary politician. So now, on this night of his death, it was in its own context rather what his great armies had been: an incomparably wide, incomparably powerful force held together by subtle, casual disciplines which no other man could have developed and which no other man could have made effective. He had made of the Democratic Party an amalgam of strength running both horizontally and vertically from Coast to Coast. He had, in fact, formed the first truly and consistently national political party that the United States had ever known. So strong had it been that through its immense power he had been able to break the most entrenched of all domestic political fortress-barriers, the barrier that *no* President should have, or even seek, a third term in office. True, this had been an action showing heavy casualties and desertions-on-principle, not only among the enlisted personnel, the voters, but also among some of the high general officers of the party, including such stalwart staff people as James A. Farley, FDR's first political operations officer and his first Postmaster General.

But to count the casualties was hardly germane to the central point. The question was not whether one would lose some of his troops; you do not even propose to storm the fortified heights of any Gettysburg without advance acknowledgment of cost. The question was whether, at *any* cost and any number of casualties, it would be possible to break a storied resistance of this kind. And FDR has shown that no position, domestically, could be defended against his assault.

So it was that until breath had left his body that afternoon in Warm Springs he had commanded what no other politician in a free society had ever so long commanded, anytime, anywhere. This was a literally irresistible political force which, while losing some of its power as the years drew on, was still without example in the history of democratic politics. This great thing he had made by acts of national leadership and national reconciliation alternating with acts of occasionally deliberate intransigence and offense against this or that class or economic group, this or that section. But the "class warfare" so often charged against him (and this was the worn and tired phrase that was most of all in the minds of some on that night of death) had had in it far less either of class or of warfare than had sometimes seemed to be the case.

For one of the glories of this man who had now gone forever from us was that he had made a political nation of what, from the onset of the Civil War, generations before, had been a series of diffuse and regional and sectional power groups and blocs only now and then drawn transiently together in political terms. To be sure, another Democratic President, Woodrow Wilson, had appealed sentimentally to the South as a part of the whole Republic. But such small success as Wilson had had toward drawing the South back into the Union had been more symbolic than real or lasting.

But the great party-political mosaic Roosevelt had made was peculiarly his personal creation, the result of his private perceptions and skills. It formed a body of which the head was now dead. And once the head had fallen, inevitable lifelessness began to spread over the trunk and arms and legs of this body. So, perhaps without being too fanciful, it could be said that the funeral train which was to bring Roosevelt's body back from Georgia to Washington the next night was somberly laden in more senses than one as it clicked quietly across the grade crossings and the switches in the little Southern towns along the way. It was to bring back the lost, dead symbol and heart of the newly national Democratic Party. It was, in a way, trailing the smoke plumes of a farewell in the nighttime to the South, which had remained, if sometimes resentfully, faithful to Roosevelt's new-old Democratic Party but would not again be so faithful for many years, and perhaps never.

Political movements, wherever they are consequential, are movements mostly of men and only secondarily of circumstances, or even issues. We are early told in childhood's civics classes, of course, that this is a government of "law and not of men." This, no doubt, is a harmless ideal; but if so it is also an idealization of reality.

For what Harry Truman was inheriting and what the Democratic Party less directly was inheriting and what the country itself was even less directly inheriting that night was the slow collapse of a great political movement which had been made by one man and could not survive its singular creator. It did not mean, of course, that now there would be no more social security, no more protection against broken banks, no more right to organize labor unions, no more of this and no more of that. These reforms would go on, of course, for they were the palpable legacies, like the stocks and bonds left to the family when a great entrepreneur comes to the end of his work on earth. What is left in the bank is still in the bank. It does not, however, follow from this that the value of the certificates, so to speak, will remain what it had been after other hands have taken over the management of the portfolio.

It did not mean that the stroke which had taken the life of Franklin Roosevelt in Warm Springs had at the same instant canceled out what was called the New Deal. But it did mean that the political structure which had made the New Deal and in turn had itself been entrenched by the New Deal was now in continued existence only in the fleeting sense that a cut-through tree remains momentarily upright until it begins slowly to topple in the forest.

It is, of course, arguable that the tree would before long have fallen anyhow. For it could be said that had it not been sawn across by Roosevelt's death it might have been sawn across, sooner or later, by the intractable alterations of history itself. And it is true, too, that the New Deal in the formulistic sense had departed already—had gone when "Dr. Win-the-War" came upon the scene. The concern here, however, is not with the New Deal as a formula or even as a fact. The concern here is with what was far more subtle and far more evanescent, the incredible political complex upon which the New Deal had rested. I do not talk here, in a word, so much of the works of the artist; I talk of the artist himself and of the frame in which he worked.

So, such thin connection as there had been, before death, between the now lifeless body of FDR and of the nervously active body of the successor President in the White House that night was now nonexistent, so far as the future of the Democratic Party was concerned. It would have been profoundly moving had one been able to look then beyond the sorrow and loss of the night and so to perceive what was now going to happen, not only to the world, not only to the country, but also to the political mechanism to which both the fallen Roosevelt and the ascending Truman were in such differing ways so committed.

For Truman, the supposedly crudely adept and practical

politician who would know little about the world's great affairs, was now to undertake a politician's task for which, actually, he was as unfitted as Roosevelt the supposed supreme internationalist had actually been unfitted to deal with the hidden but basic issues of war strategy and postwar peace.

Do I mean to say, then, that the life preparation of Groton and Harvard and long acquaintance with the world's great had somehow not equipped Roosevelt so well for the world of global politics as Truman had been equipped by little formal education and the mores of the provincial Southwestern town of Independence, Missouri? And do I mean to say that Roosevelt, to whom the term magnificence was not inapplicable, understood ordinary ward and boss politics far better than the grayish, unimpressive man who owed his very start to the ugly local machine of old Boss Tom Pendergast in Kansas City? Yes, in both cases.

For all of this, the years were to bring, to those able to comprehend that outrageous paradox really exists, certain irrefutable proofs.

Truman was inheriting that night a Democratic Party fatally wrenched about by the loss of its irreplaceable leader, as well as a broken grand policy for liquidating the war and consolidating the peace in Western interests. But as he set out gropingly upon his way, the first steps he would take on the party problem (and all subsequent steps, indeed) would show a surprising inability to grapple with its most elementary realities. And the first steps he would take upon the grand postwar problem would show an amazing ability to perceive (or, if one prefers, to let the preceptions of others have their way with his mind) the deepest realities of that problem.

Roosevelt, the true pragmatist, had made the New Deal because it was right and needed *for the time in which he made it.* He had no slightest hesitation in casting it away, as an artisan casts away a hammer when a saw becomes more needed in his task, when he thought its work had been done. That is, he was moving rightward in his thinking as the war drew to its close because he knew that the preconditions for the New Deal existed no longer and so were not really relevant any longer. He knew that the banks were now open and not closed. He knew that the soup kitchens were now closed and not open. He knew, indeed, that the country which a few years beforehand had been so tragically in want of things would now become overfull of things, gross and bloated with them, if truth be told. Had he lived, there is little doubt that he would have begun to move openly, with that cheerfully intuitive way of his, to redress the balance. There were now very few forgotten men, just as there were now very few unemployed men. The problem no longer was one of hunger marchers nor with the erstwhile suppressed millions. Now the real problem was not to let the new materialism of the many vulgarize the country and weaken its power and purposes as the old materialism of the few—the "money changers" of the past—had mocked and perverted the country's ideals in the years before the New Deal.

Chapter

Nine

The great central point was that the President who was now dead had for twelve years maintained the most complicated possible political organization in a uniquely exquisite balance. His essential purposes, beginning with the First Hundred Days of the New Deal, had put upon him the absolute necessity of raising a movement of a deliberately overstated mass kind of democracy for which in any ordinary times the country would have been far from ready and from which he himself would in ordinary times surely have recoiled. He was dealing here with mammoth and unexampled economic circumstances, which were far more than merely "problems." They were deadly perilous realities which for the first time had brought clearly into question the whole basic assumption that our national life should and could be based on the system of liberal, capitalistic democracy. The enemies of this notion were not men so much as the fortuities and accidents and necromancies of trade and currency. But because to the average man these enemies were so unknown and so utterly unknowable, Roosevelt had recognized that they could not be grappled with unless he could put into the people an unparalleled sense of political community and indeed of political communion. All had lost their way in the dark forests; to lead men so lost, the first necessity is to make them grasp their hands together and then to take them forward—forward into whatever, but forward at all cost. For they must not be allowed simply to mill around in the dark. They must not be left to fear "fear itself."

But such great joining of hands—under the symbol of the NRA Blue Eagle; under this, that and the other symbol—is not wise or needful in *all* circumstances. Of this Roosevelt had always been fully aware—not to mention the fact that such joining also *was never to his personal taste*. This "revolutionary"—and how extremely odd that many so thought of him on that night of his death and still so think of him—was a million light-years from some bearded Trotsky. The great estate at Hyde Park had hardly prepared him to appreciate the dank cellars of "social protest," and all that. Even the "planned-economy" economists, who were seen by many as absolutely swarming over Washington and the whole countryside with their dangerous arcane nostrums, had only been gallantly borne and ungladly suffered by FDR in the interest of the cause. They bored him, as so close and perceptive an FDR associate as Francis Biddle once told me. They bored him—not to tears, but rather to rude outcries once they had left the Presidential presence.

In a word, the great Democratic mass (and democratic mass) had been assembled by Roosevelt simply to enable him to do certain things at certain times. They had not been brought together—indeed his whole complex of leadership had not been brought together—in the tremulous spirit of the True Believer and in order solely to promote the interests of that person whom Henry Wallace chose to call, so often, the Common Man. Roosevelt's interest was in man, not common man; it was in *American* man and not in man in the whole universe. And his own, private mind was much less than deeply moved by the orotund, evangelical quality of the slo-

gans which were used by many—and also by him—to promote
the quite practical aspirations that lay in his quite cool mind.

All the same, to do what he had done in the first phases
of his long administration he had allowed himself to become
publicly an indispensable part and a symbol of certain sen-
timentalisms to which he had to give free play simply in order
to raise and maintain the wide political structure which he
so needed for his purposes. On this very day of his death in
Georgia, some of the resulting complications were becoming
apparent. Though there were no longer any really "forgotten
men," many of the Roosevelt associates were still refusing
to forget those who had already been amply remembered.
Among Catholics, there is the saying that the convert to
Rome often becomes more Catholic than the Pope. So it was
that many of the Rooseveltians became more Rooseveltian
than Roosevelt this because his was always a strictly pragmatic approach whereas theirs was an approach of a feverish
idealism, almost of a religiosity, a secular piety, a scrupulosity,
so to speak. (What price the sneers of these same men a long
time later when a certain General Eisenhower was running
a political campaign under the title of "Crusade"? Who was
it who had first put "crusade" into our modern politics?)

Had the dead leader, then, really not been "sincere"? Was
he "cynical," and lacking in "ideals"? Of course, he was sincere. He was simply not bemused. He had always reckoned
—and entirely correctly, for in the true fundamentals he was
a man of tradition—that his job was a *political* job, not a
moralistic job. Among the things one could honestly say of
him—that night, and always—was this: He had no cant in him
—or no more than was absolutely necessary to perform his
highest duties. Still the very vastness of the political instrumentality he had prepared, with the official Democratic Party

as its nexus but by no means its whole, carried within itself the seeds of its own destruction, now that he was no longer on hand to check their growth.

For the surviving heirs of the Administration (Truman was no heir but rather only the Constitutional accident to whom fell the country's headship) had learned from FDR both too much and too little. They knew how he had prepared the great party monolith, and how and where and why he had applied his various cements. They knew, and in the academic sense sometimes better even than he, how to gather up all the discontented and the dispossessed. But, unlike FDR, they missed this overmastering point: The discontented and the dispossessed had largely vanished, long before Roosevelt's life itself had drawn to its tired and painful end.

So, from the onset of the new Administration the old New Dealers were to talk a language which was not only alien to Truman but which, quite naturally, was positively repellent to him. For he and FDR, despite all their night-and-day differences, had one great quality in common: They were both authentic men of politics; not of "idealism," and not even of ideology except insofar as ideology could be made the implement, momentary or otherwise, of their jobs in politics. One thing at least they together knew: that the first and cardinal and sovereign task of a President is to govern. The surviving New Dealers had believed, instead (and still really do) that somehow the first task is to think and to feel, to have not the right techniques but the right notions and emotions. Those who love the people this way love the people too much—and also too little. There is a stickiness in them, in political terms, anyhow. For in a parliamentary society the people are more properly and more wisely *used* than loved by the representative head—used, to be sure, for their own and the national good, but used all the same.

But though Truman had this sound instinct for the business, as had the man he now succeeded, what was possible in the way of party governance for the old President would be inevitably impossible for the new.

For this night of a great changing of the guard in the White House was, among other things, the beginning also of a long night of the long knives, within the new Administration itself and within the Roosevelt-Democratic Party. (It was to precede yet another night of the long knives—this one of Republican knives honed up for Truman and the new Truman-Democratic Party. But this latter would in some ways be actually a manifestation of secondary importance.) From the moment Truman took the oath of his office, his untenability as party leader, as distinguished from as President would be a fact foregone and sealed.

The special personality of Franklin D. Roosevelt—and this point is of a matchless importance—was the vital fluid, the very juice of life, of his party. He had held powerful men and forces in it, often not because of his own policies but even *in spite* of those policies; he had been a kind of *grand seigneur* or patron-boss to it. To millions, *he* had been its true *raison d'être*. The right-wing Southerners, increasingly appalled at much that he did, had nevertheless stayed Democratic—even though Roosevelt, and more particularly Mrs. Roosevelt, had persistently outraged their deepest feelings and prejudices in matters like the race issue.

The liberals—authentic ones, emotion-washed ones, practical ones, starry-eyed ones, the amateur liberals, the professional liberals—had been so desperately constant in their support of him as sometimes (though not constantly) to make Roosevelt himself rather desperate for some salty no-saying from those around him. They had stayed with him in sunshine and in rain and in all the variations of political weather in between. To be "for Roosevelt" became, for these, not simply a matter of choice but a matter of historical necessity and a special cachet in itself.

To them the word l-i-b-e-r-a-l had an automatic alternative spelling, R-o-o-s-e-v-e-l-t. There were in all the country only two political groups who ever had any trouble in making up their minds about FDR: these liberals, and the Republican and right-wing Democratic contingent. The Roosevelt liberals for the most part had backed the President when in the late Thirties he had opened what was in any rational theory a profoundly illiberal attack (but in practice a perfectly justified one) upon the integrity of the Supreme Court. Their rationale in all this was expressed with their characteristic cloudy melodrama and grandiosity of phrase. His rationale was in the quite simple form that is natural to all highly expert strategists, whether in politics or in war: He felt it absolutely necessary that the Court's mind be changed, simply because he thought it was a mind obsessed with the past. And, of course, change it he did; he lost the battle to pack the Court's membership but he won the war to alter its intellectual direction. At any rate, the Roosevelt liberals who had remained with him in this enterprise, the most supremely pragmatic to which he ever addressed himself, had also stayed with him when, about 1939, he calmly put aside all real thought of liberal reform and innovation and began to prepare his followers for the Second World War.

These people were bound to the man who had died that day in Warm Springs with hoops of gossamer form but of incredible strength. There were many of these hoops; some were entirely plausible, and some were merely, and oddly, psychological. But the point is that all of them were unbelievably strong. The nature of some of these psychological bonds was not the least of the explanations of the depth of the shock being felt on that night. It was here that the true, the genuine, father image was actually dashed to earth in the stupendous fact, the measureless tragedy to many, of the death of this man. For Roosevelt was in sober truth far more of the "father" to millions than Dwight Eisenhower was ever going to be much farther along in time.

The theory of Eisenhower as projecting the father image was great nonsense. The image he would project would be one of the successful executive, the embodiment of one American dream and legend—the senior vice-president of the big bank who moves into a neighborhood in suburbia where the next most distinguished resident is not even yet an assistant executive. I do not sneer at this regard; for so far as it went it was quite genuine and quite understandable. But the warm response to a man like Eisenhower because he had reached a great success and withal bore his honors with cheerful unostentation and with a total sense of participation in the strictly middle-class attitudes of the community, was an infinite distance from a response to the image of the "father."

For the father is not merely loved; he is loved as a superior being, never as an equal, and never as just a jolly good fellow. And to many, Roosevelt really and truly was the father in this authentic definition—or, as I have suggested earlier on, the shepherd among the sheep but, by definition, not himself *of* the sheep.

So it was that in the loss of FDR many had lost something which they never could have defined but something whose absence they felt none the less keenly in an ache of the spirit. To some it meant the departure of a man who with classic skill had saved a country's life at home. To some it was rather more complicated than this; it meant the departure of a man who in accomplishing all this immense work had also given to other able and decent men—the academic types, for illustration—a real and honorable and useful place for the first time in the nation's public life. And into the bargain he had shown them a subtle kind of leadership which while really of the one-man sort had permitted a flowering of their talents and an earned sense of value to the Republic itself. It was not merely that the dead President had brought the intellectuals into government; he had vindicated their way of life; he had listened to them, at least sometimes, when they were right. And he had set in motion a process—a marriage, or at any rate a good and satisfying liaison betwixt Academe and national politics—that still unfolds to enrich and enliven both the university and the national political community. He had done more, too, than greatly to encourage the pursuit of that harsh and difficult and rewarding art which is, curiously, called "political science." He had made it possible for the political scientists and the historians and biographers to climb periodically down from the towers of ivory to make genuinely read (and thus real) contributions to the long serial story of our corporate life as a nation. It seems to me, in passing, that what FDR had brought about here gave ample cause for mourning that night amongst those who had benefited from it and would benefit from it as, in their separate ways, they were in turn to benefit all the rest of us. To bring forward even a handful of men—Arthur M. Schlesinger, Jr., and Walt Rostow and others of their like—is no inconsiderable thing in itself. And I say it as one who has no difficulty in disagreeing often with the Schlesingers, and their associates.

Chapter

Ten

But yet another of the gossamer-steel hoops binding the dead President to the living was at once far more complicated and far less desirable, than all these others. For one of the factors that had made FDR an irreplaceable, if lofty, father to some was his unwitting appeal to a very involved kind of snobbism in them. This would have an instantly ill effect upon the Democratic Party, post-Roosevelt, and on the small and shaken but sturdily courageous man called Truman who was now so tentatively occupying that strange place, the White House. This snobbism—I could illustrate it with the names of some of its holders but I will not—expressed itself in a feeling of happiness just to be *with* Roosevelt, whether close to him or only in that interminable queue of followers stretching out into the far distances.

Because they thought him to be "an aristocrat"—which, of course, this scion of a sturdy and essentially mercantile upper-middle-class family never was—they felt a transference of aristocratic status to themselves simply by the fact of being in his company. They would turn at once and with a peculiar savagery, in a kind of shrill contempt for his presumably low social status, upon Harry Truman. It is easy to forget in retrospect. But the fact is that the first gaps in what should normally have been great Democratic support for the new President, so heavily burdened as he was at best, were opened by defections from among the snob-Rooseveltians. It is not now widely recalled. But the killing epithet, "that little man," was of snob-Democratic, and not Republican, origin. Indeed the destruction of Truman's essential domestic political base was begun by the same people and not by the Republicans. These latter came only later on the scene of attack.

For all these reasons, then—because he could not appeal even dimly to the snob-liberal Democrats; because his competence was at first understandably suspect even among the sensible liberal Democrats—Truman's place as party controller was to be mortgaged before he had learned which room was which in the White House. The whisper that he was not only a humble man but somehow also a rather *low* man was going around Washington before the Roosevelt funeral train had started for Washington from Georgia.

It may be that there was some remote parallel in Truman's curious situation with that of Andrew Johnson of Tennessee when, nearly a century before, he had succeeded the martyred Lincoln. Johnson, a Border State man too, was thought of as an extraordinary common man; though God knows his late chief, Lincoln, had been also considered one. But whatever quasi-parallel did exist was at best thin in the extreme; even our snobberies had become much complicated in the years between the last days of the Civil War and the last days of the Second World War.

Roosevelt himself, to his unending private amusement, had become a snob symbol of two wholly different kinds: If the social climbers in his own train had rushed to identify themselves with him, so other social climbers had fled from him in fear that somehow they would not seem anti-Roosevelt enough to suit their private necessities. I remember a little dinner party before the war, in Westchester County, New York, in which this alternate kind of snobbism was peculiarly illustrated. Westchester County was the home of a prewar gray flannel suit long before Mr. Sloan Wilson's novel about the man in such a suit had become a part of our social folklore. In those days I thought of Westchester—and unwisely said as much sometimes while riding the commuters' train to and from Grand Central Station—as the home of the secondhand-station-wagon set. The 1940 Presidential campaign was approaching its frenetic climax while Wendell Willkie, Roosevelt's Republican antagonist, was rushing about the country calling for the salvation of something he called the "Amur-rican" way of life. Earnest Republican ladies from the suburbs were writing to the papers that there were only so many more days (before the election) in which to save that way of life. Upon inquiry as to my own intentions in this matter of national rescue, I told my dinner companions calmly that I intended to vote again for Roosevelt. They were aghast; but the kinder among them were ready to forgive and forget on the theory that, as a Southerner, I could so vote, not quite rationally but not, anyhow, was an outrageous or "unbearable" irrationality, because of a tragic sectional inheritance in the blood for which I was not really to blame.

But one chap there found it quite too much. "But," he told me, "people of *our* class *can't* vote for that man." "Little fellow," I said to him, "what the hell is *our* class? *I* am a newspaperman. If I owned an electric utility company I don't mind saying I probably wouldn't be for Roosevelt. And what is *your* class, by the way?" It turned out he was really a glorified teller in a Manhattan bank—some sort of third vice-president.

Perhaps it sounds altogether too pat. But the plain fact is that on that night of FDR's death, sitting alone after my work in the bar at the National Press Club in Washington where several others, too, were sitting quietly and also alone, mem-

ories of Roosevelt and of my own father became mixed and
merged in my mind. (Of how many other men must this
have been true that night!) I thought of how Roosevelt would
have laughed—throwing back that massive head now never
to move again, either in gaiety or in anger—had he ever
been told of that conversation at the dinner table in Scarsdale.
I thought, too, of my own father, already dead these many
years, and how he would chuckle over the professional Southern aristocrats who in my youth were forever calling upon
him not to forget that "we people of the *old* Southern families" had duties to a "way of life" that had died in agony
before he and they were ever born. (He respected this agony;
but he could read a calendar, too.) I knew at that moment
in the Press Club, as so many of us must have known in
many places, that in one night a man could lose his father
twice.

Truman, however, was losing not a father; but only a fair
chance to try fully to succeed a party leader who had done
his work so well and so personally that the work could not
really go forward in other hands.

As Vice-President he had been excluded not only from the
great and inner realities of government but also from any
kind of effective participation in the direction of his own
party. He had come to the office at a lift of Roosevelt's
beckoning finger. The Big Man, busy with the cares of the
war, in 1944 had done at least this much for the future: He
had, if rather absent-mindedly, made some rational provision
for the eventualities of a succession on which his mind never
cared much to dwell.

In 1940 FDR's crisply sensitive political antennae had informed him that the challenge of Willkie posed far different
problems than had Hoover in 1932 and Alf Landon of Kansas
in 1936. For, beginning with Willkie's nomination in 1940,

the Republican Party had committed itself to a stupendous change of mind and purpose. It had been necessary to put the Old Guard to death at last. The G.O.P. had resolved, though denying it all at every step of the way, that it must alter itself fundamentally amidst the realities of the new world if ever it was to come to national power again. (Speaking of "revolutions," this was one measure of the profundity in domestic political terms of the revolution which the dead President had made.) So Willkie came forward as the first of the "modern" Republicans; and the locus of power of the Republican Party was radically shifted from the Midwest to the Eastern seaboard—shifted for many years to come, and perhaps forever.

With Willkie as his adversary, FDR had looked about him, smelt the national air, tested it with his wetted finger, and brought in Henry Wallace to run with him. The notion was simply this: Already Roosevelt, putting first things first as he always did, had begun himself to turn from reform to a consolidation both of his own political power and of the country's slowly rising military power. So now he needed a campaign associate who could most strongly appeal to the dedicated and professional liberals in whom Roosevelt himself had largely lost interest. No doubt FDR was aware of their continued peculiar and unshakable enchantment with him; but to be on the safe side he gave them Wallace as a kind of sentimental token that the one true faith was not being abandoned. Wallace had fitted the 1940 bill exactly. He was so "liberal" that, as the saying goes, it wasn't even true. Roosevelt, of course, paid precisely no attention to Wallace after the election—as later he paid precisely none to Truman.

But when 1944 came along Wallace simply wouldn't do. The slow Roosevelt turn rightward—to repeat, a turn made simply for pragmatic reasons and not for reasons bound up in that word Roosevelt never really liked, the word "ideological"—made it inconceivable to risk leaving the country in Wallace's honorable but quite buttery hands. Byrnes wouldn't do for 1944 for two reasons: First, he was too important to be fobbed off in an office that had no meaning whatever to FDR except for the possibility of his own death. (Roosevelt had viewed the Vice-President, correctly, much as he had quite incorrectly viewed the United States Senate, as a rather useless and annoying appendage so long as all went well with his own life.) Second, Byrnes was a Southerner, and this might mean turning too much to the right too soon. Truman, for his part, was moderately acceptable in Roosevelt's reckoning. He was, Heaven knows, no Henry Wallace. On the other hand, he was no Southerner, and he was, as Roosevelt knew, a good working politician, if never in the same league in this skill as that of the Old Master.

Thus Truman had got the job much as a man might be plucked from a line of applicants at an employment office. So far, so good. But once Truman had got the job, FDR was through with all that business. As he had been his own Secretary of State, of War, and so on, so he had been his own Vice-President. He knew who Truman was, of course. But Truman, notwithstanding all the adjectives connoting combat—"scrappy," "fighter," and so on, that later were to be applied to him—was something else, too. In some ways, in spite of his fabulous cussing ability and his ready use of four-letter words, he was far more bound to the genteel tradition than was his chief. For one illustration, Truman had never pushed himself in where he felt unwanted. And so he had never sought to thrust himself into the real operating centers of a party of which he was, all the same, presumably a considerable official.

He had an involvement in the Democratic Party of Roosevelt primarily because he was almost religiously simply a *Democrat*, a total partisan, in domestic terms, by inheritance much as a man is, say, unthinkingly and totally an Episcopalian or a Presbyterian. Secondarily Truman's involvement with the Roosevelt-Democratic Party was through his devotion to the policies of that party, toward which he looked emotionally as a Fundamentalist looks at some such concept as baptism by total immersion. Roosevelt, however, had never been solely or even primarily a Democrat; he had been a virtuoso *politician* to whom the Democratic Party was simply a mechanism and nothing more. To Roosevelt, Democratic Party policies had been far from immutable and far from sacrosanct. They had in fact been mere means toward ends which in his mind—and quite soundly, too—were constantly altering, in minor or major ways, as time went on and as national necessities were themselves altering in degree or in principle.

It was this quite sunny and quite open pragmatism of Roosevelt's that had made it possible for him to bring together and to keep together such motley and disparate groups as made up *his* Democratic Party. Men who disagreed would go along with Roosevelt the politician because he was amiably and comfortably free of that strong touch of political Puritanism which, sometimes hypocritically and sometimes with deadly honesty, has characterized most of the history of our public life.

They would on the whole go along with him because, while he was, at this or that phase of his administration, committed to policies they might fear or detest, they were always aware, if sometimes only subconsciously so, that Roosevelt was not necessarily and mortally and forever committed and so could and would change his mind if occasion arose. He had never looked at politics as an exercise in high dogma; he had not looked upon this or that policy as a changeless expression of revealed truth. In a word, he was not all that "sincere"—and it was a godsend that he was not, in those years when he was feeling his way through the terrible domestic sicknesses which had fallen upon us. Good politicians—and of these there are not very many and never have been—are deeply distrustful of that sort of "sincerity," just as they draw back in skepticism and distaste from all those who prate of "spiritual values" in political life. For, speaking plainly, there are as such no universally agreed "spiritual values" in most public issues. That is to say, there is the greatest danger in attempting to associate spiritual considerations with public affairs and to make grand, final personal judgments as to what governmental attitude is adequately "spiritual" or "good" and what governmental attitude is crassly secular or "evil."

There is the profoundest of wisdom in the Biblical injunction about rendering to Caesar the things that are Caesar's. As an old political writer I never knew a politician given to making stirring moral judgments out loud who could be trusted very far. It is not that all these fellows are cant-ridden; it is only that at best they operate in a hopeless confusion of purposes. Theirs is the worst of all public sins—ineptitude.

Now, Harry Truman sitting so alone and so troubled in the White House that night was not preparing to set off—and did not set off—as a fantastically and overly "principled" new President to carry through the old and already shifting Roosevelt policies as a kind of holy war of obligation. Nor was he, as the new head of the Democratic Party, awash with evangelistic impracticalities. All the same, his view of the burden laid upon him was somewhat oversimplified. He *was* much more "sincere" than Roosevelt had been; and as it was to turn out this was a great pity.

Chapter

Eleven

For Truman would set out, as to domestic problems, upon a course that assumed the inviolability of policies which Roosevelt in his mind had already been tossing aside as no longer needed or germane to the new situation of the country. The new President's first message to Congress would call for a "twenty-one point" program of social legislation which would have gone far beyond Roosevelt and would have much out-New-Dealed the old New Deal itself. This message would take no account whatever of the plain fact that national necessities and national attitudes and national desires had vastly changed as the war went on and then drew to its close. Truman's first effort would be to drive markedly to the left a country already determined to go rightward and actually *already, long since, moving in that direction.* The fact that Congress—and a Democratic Congress at that—was instantly to show that it would do nothing whatever toward such a program was to be damaging enough to the Truman Presidency.

Far more damaging, however, to Truman as the new party leader would be the resulting and dramatically demonstrated disruptive effect upon his leadership. For a leader to fail in his demands upon his followers is bad enough. But so to fail, in circumstances where it is patent to the smallest follower that the Boss has wholly misread all political reality in the first place, is even worse. The maintenance of party discipline, even in the most favorable of fortunes, would have been difficult for Truman. In the circumstances that now were to unfold, it was to become wholly impossible. He needed most of all to relax his legislative demands; instead he would only increase them. He needed first of all to establish his personal headship over the party; instead he would move first of all to institutionalize rather than to personalize that headship.

The fact that he was an infinitely bigger man inside than he ever looked outside—that he was, indeed, a truly and deeply *modest* man—was going to have to be dragged out of him by still-distant future events and almost against his will. Never, one would be able to say in truth later, had a man so doggedly hidden from the public the greatness that was in him. But in the hours of measureless change in the evening and on the morrow of an old President's passing the new President was burdened by the most attractive of all faults and the most endearing of all shortcomings: All that was in him forbade him to seize aggressively (and with that blandly ruthless and incomparably useful ambition that had lain in his dead predecessor) the primacy of this land which he ought really to have seized at every cost.

So began the process by which Truman's inherent power as party leader began to melt away even before the funeral lines were to be said in the White House for a leader, and for a phase in history, that had gone forever. So began the dissolution of the Roosevelt-Democratic Party, that crazy, that powerful, *magnum opus* of one man; that first—and possibly that last—truly national party ever to sprawl in weight and wonder across all the United States.

And as the crumbling went forward it was to become more and more apparent that Roosevelt's great political pragmatism, for all its common-sense utility, had not been quite pragmatic enough, considering his own mortality. In war he had not recognized that defeating the enemy was not the sole answer; had not grasped that the kind of peace we were to have was a consideration equally as important as attaining a peace. So, in domestic politics he had not sensed that mere victories on the running issues of his days would not sustain the political instrumentality he had so brilliantly built. Many times he had overcome his political opposition and he had made his new party by shining tours de force—and sometimes by harsh measures, indeed.

He was in one sense an amiable bully as a public man and he was aware that when a leader feels compelled in crisis to use his followers and opponents roughly there will be accounts to be paid when the storm has passed. Men will accept this treatment when they must; but they will think, at least, of squaring the account later, if not actually and actively of revenge itself.

He had at times used these opponents and critics very hardly. His own mastery of his political mechanism had been so intimate, and so sensitive, that *so long as he lived* he could maintain it, by loosening this screw or that screw when the pressure became intolerable on this or that group or faction or point of view within the national community. But the Constitutional successor, Truman, could not operate (and no conceivable successor for that matter could have operated) these controls as could the man who had created and embodied them.

So the Democratic Party, post-Roosevelt, was to begin to fragment under Truman's hand before FDR had been two months in his grave in the ordered beauty of Hyde Park upon the Hudson. The King was dead; the successor King, in this sense, was no King at all. And the Republicans had waited very long to give their retort in history to the era of Frank-

lin Roosevelt. Now, sore from having been beaten so often
and so long by the incomplete genius, FDR, they would fall
to with understandable vigor (and often with entirely im-
permissible savagery) to pay back the score.

Truman was thus placed, from the very hour he entered
the White House that late afternoon as its new master, under
heavy fire from two directions: from dissident Democrats
who reckoned to overcome him who had succeeded the man
they never could overcome; from Republicans who reckoned
on about the same thing.

Thus was to begin the somber overture to a true American
tragedy. This was not simply the withering away of a tremendous political-party instrumentality, for there was nothing
at all timeless about *that*. It was the withering away instead of
the power of an American White House at a time of long,
compelling, accumulating crisis in the life of this country.

The nation was emerging from the war with a sense of
rootlessness, and even of a certain vulgar and unlettered cynicism, into a time of far too much material possession and
far too little moral authority at the top. (It should never be
forgotten that all that is good in our system rests upon a
moral authority which is not religious in connotation but
which is also not a mere compendium or tabulation of such
votes as may be cast by a majority of the people. The Constitution, the Bill of Rights, the true, inner purpose of the
Republic and its reason for being, are not expressed by majorities, large or small; they live upon an ancient concept of
the right relationship between the leader and the led, the state
and the man, which has nothing whatever to do with Gallup
polls.)

The true sadness that was now coming upon us, a far more
profound sadness than was involved in the arrival of death
at Warm Springs, was this: The moral authority of a new

President of the United States was going to be wholly compromised, and at home destroyed, in part because of blind circumstances and in part because the dead leader had been unable so to plan and prepare as to enable his successor to maintain the party structure which was the indispensable base of that Presidential posture the country so urgently and so bitterly now required.

Any successor President would have needed both great luck and great strength within his own party to withstand the counterforces which were now gathering in determination to get a bit of their own back from the most fabulously successful and powerful politician and political movement in our history.

It was, by necessity, upon Truman that these forces were to center; Roosevelt through fate had cheated them of their chance to turn the tables upon him. Their hands had been stayed by unending crises; first the Depression, then the war. Now, they thought, as the war drew to an end, their time had come. But FDR had again passed from their effective reach, this time forever. The man now lying dead in the cottage at Warm Springs had not only left his designated successor unaware of the presence of the most awful power in history, the nuclear power which was soon to open a new age of man. He had also, though not in this instance by choice, left that successor to fight, without real political weapons, the last rear-guard actions of a dying New Deal whose creator would have been both prepared and able to liquidate it in order. Truman was to be neither so prepared nor so able.

The Roosevelt-Democratic Party had, in the moment of the last spasm of an overloaded heart, actually become something else entirely: Now it was simply a *Democratic* party, which was tired both of glory and of combat; resentful in part of its own past successes; doubtful in part of the rightness of some of those very successes, mindful in part of the harsh means-to-ends that its old leader had so often and so unworriedly employed; distrustful in part of the validity of its own achievements insofar as these had sometimes been obtained by questionable means; inescapably worried in part by awareness that much tradition—and some of it sound tradition —had been cast aside or trampled underfoot incontinently. Great generals who die in the last battle live forever; great generals who survive all battles live to see an end of all the glory and to be caught up in sterile disputes in their clubs, where old men in dull mufti fight over and over again the lost and forgotten actions of the past.

In all our history we had had two Presidents, and two alone, whose whole Administrations, whose whole public lives, had been totally interlinked with truly mortal struggles within their country—Lincoln in the crisis of the War Between the States and slavery; Roosevelt in the crisis of the Depression and then the crisis of the Second World War. Had Lincoln lived it is more than possible that he would have been able to reunite in true peace the nation whose legal union he had maintained in civil war. No one else could possibly have done this, for Lincoln's work had been the work not of a party, not even of a government, but of a man, peculiarly and providentially fitted for the burdens that were laid upon him. Roosevelt, given continued life, might have brought the country out upon a new plateau, might have accommodated its new domestic problems, might have given a new rationale to his own political movement that would have kept it going on strongly, if in new directions. And he might even have somehow found a way to reclaim the great foreign-policy errors which had so limited his military victory, though one cannot in retrospect greatly credit that possibility. But he was now dead, and not alive; he had served his great purpose and he had gone before the time of testing could come for much of what he had done and not done. He had fallen in the last battle. And it was left for another, and not for him, to fight over and over again the lost actions of the past.

The people themselves sensed vaguely that night, or so I believe, something of the new air that was blowing across this land—the new air that was so shortly to transform this country's political purposes from the gay reformism of the Thirties to the grayer and soberer and wiser—and also more selfish—political centralism of the immediate and later postwar periods. This is in part why there was such an indescribable poignance in the mood of farewell; for it was farewell to our most stirring as well as our most worrying memories, our memories of storm and strife, yes, but also of high days of hope and action—always of action and yet more action. It was, in a way, farewell to a part of our youth, with all its trials and dangers—but also its irreplaceable dash and glamour. When the first sad bulletin had come that late afternoon from Warm Springs we had passed in a moment from young manhood to middle age.

In a far more measurable and palpable sense the new master of the White House, Truman, had every reason that night for the dread and anxiety that lay upon him.

The left wing of the party Roosevelt had commanded was already—and increasingly—disenchanted with the directions he had lately been taking. The right wing, which Roosevelt had held in control by personal qualities which could never be transferred to another, was already moving restively away from the strange house he had built. The handwriting was truly upon the wall. Within nineteen months the Democrats, under a leadership so suddenly thrust upon an ill-prepared Truman, would lose the first national election they had lost since 1928—that for the Eightieth Congress. This election would be seen in the afterlight to have been many things, most discernibly a popular revulsion from one of the wartime controls, that on red meat, which typified so much of Roosevelt's economic policy both in the Depression period and the war period. (A country already superlatively well-fed, surely by the standards of the millions then starving in Europe and Asia, was to decide that its government was allowing it to feed too poorly.)

And this election was to open upon our national stage a new drama, a bitter drama, and one so very different from those we had known since "Happy Days Are Here Again" had keynoted the Roosevelt victory over the decent and the politically inept Herbert Hoover in 1932. For what we were now to see, beginning with the Eightieth Congress, was an unexampled attack upon the Roosevelt era by the Republican opposition and the right-wing Democrats. The brave but politically ill-armed Truman would pay heavily (and the country would pay heavily) for the wrongs—and also the rights—of the era of Franklin D. Roosevelt.

To be sure, it would be logically possible to put the 1946 Congressional election down as a tired aberration of a tired country; but it was also to be far more than this. For it was to be in this Eightieth Congress—that despised "worst Congress," as Truman was later to call it—that the opposition was to mount a series of counteroffensives which would destroy Truman's domestic leadership, complete the destruction of the Democratic Party of Roosevelt's time, and forbid the government of the United States to take its rightful place of leadership in a postwar world filled with dangers scarcely less acute than those which Hitler himself had created.

What was shortly to come was what might be called the era of Taft—of Senator Robert A. Taft, the courageous, the honorable, the surpassingly wrongheaded man who was lead-

ing the decent part of the Republican Party's understandable
drive to reclaim the country from what it honestly believed
to have been the evil excesses of the Roosevelt time. Taft
himself was not personally to succeed; he was never to grasp
the Presidential nomination of his own party. But the forces
he was to set in motion—which were to give cover to other
and dark forces symbolized by the Joseph McCarthys of the
end of the decade of 1940 and the beginning of the decade
of 1950—were to give a destructive reply in history to the
era of Roosevelt.

True, Truman was to be elected in his own right in 1948.
But it would become entirely plain, later on, that this did
not mean that the Roosevelt-Democratic Party still lived. In
that very campaign the break-up was to be illustrated with
harsh drama by the defection from Truman of the two ex-
tremes—the Henry Wallaceites on the one side, the Southern
Bourbons on the other side. It was to be, indeed, an election
not won by Truman and the Democrats but rather lost by
the incredibly clumsy campaign of Thomas E. Dewey for
the Republicans. (This was to be the man, Dewey, who
would later be seen as one of the worst possible candidates
and one of the ablest possible candidate-makers in the history
of the Republican Party.) And Truman himself was to return to office under a drumfire of attack which would rise to
so savage a crescendo by the end of his last term as to leave
him powerless to run the affairs of his party or the domestic
affairs of his country, but still able to do one thing of a
certain value: to save the whole Western world from that
encroachment of imperialist Communism, beginning with the
salvation of Greece and Turkey, to which Roosevelt had
laid it open. The Democratic Party in its unique Roosevelt
form, to repeat, began to die on the very night so many were
mourning the death of its architect and operator. The coun-

try was left without a strong political party anywhere on the horizon and without a strong political leader anywhere at all. But it did have this: It had, in the new and unostentatious man in the White House, a great *President*, a rarely-matched President, a simple man who was to be able to do so much more—and so much less—than had his extraordinary predecessor.

So it was Roosevelt the all-too-fallible, as well as Roosevelt the matchless, for whom the tears of so many were being shed, in actuality or in the heart of this nation, on that memorable night of April 12, 1945.

Chapter

Twelve

Just past midnight in Warm Springs on the very early morning of April 13, 1945, Franklin Roosevelt's body lay in a great bronze coffin in the Little White House. Harry Truman had arranged to have Mrs. Roosevelt flown down to this place of her husband's death. The sense of astonishment that Roosevelt was gone was all but universal in this country and in the world. It had been, however, an event not wholly unexpected to those who had been very close to the President. Many eminent men were later to write of their memories of his sadly faltering powers. Much was to be said, and said again, of the ethics of his decision to seek a fourth term, as though he must have known, even back in 1944, that his powers were failing him. For my own part I most recall simply what my friend Grace Tully, his confidential secretary, told me long later. She did not dramatize her recollections. Nor did she pass any kind of judgment on the man or his motives; she had loved the one and she passionately respected the other, his motives.

"Along toward the end," she recalled, "the President would nod occasionally while he was dictating *and just seem to go away* for a moment or two. Then his head would snap up, like a man who had awakened from the very briefest of cat naps, and he would go on with his dictating unaware that for that little time *he had gone away*."

99

Gone away.

This short, unpretentious phrase expressed it all in the darkness of that predawn in Warm Springs. This was one of the immense dramas in our history; but it was a drama much played down, a drama suitable to the smallness, the humbleness, of the place in which the President had died. FDR himself, with an unconscious and unintended fitness, had laid down his great task and his great power with very small and homely final acts as head of state. One of these, with singular aptness, had been his signature of a bill to continue the life of the Commodity Credit Corporation and to increase its borrowing power. It was the last Act of Congress he was ever to make law; to the end his hand had been turned toward what was always in his heart his first and greatest task, the promotion of the internal affairs of the United States of America. He had died, as he had lived, as the Conservator.

In Washington General George C. Marshall, the Army Chief of Staff, was making arrangements for a military funeral. Outside the cottage in Warm Springs, as day broke, men of the services were assembling to stand the honor guard when, a few hours later, the body was to be brought down and put upon the funeral train.

Mrs. Roosevelt emerged from the cottage that morning erect and composed as always. The United States Army Band from Fort Benning, Georgia, the home of the queen of battles, the infantry, raised a dirge in the thin spring air. Much of the "brass" was there—generals and admirals and others who had marshaled this military force of two thousand men to give the traditional and long-familiar but nevertheless moving salute of farewell to a dead Commander in Chief. The colors of the infantrymen flew mourning streamers. As the body was brought down the hill from the cottage in which Roosevelt had died, the drums rolled in sad and muffled splendor. The procession paused for a moment before Georgia Hall in Warm Springs. All the patients of the Warm Springs Polio Foundation, to which FDR had so long given so much support, stood in tears before the Hall. A Georgia Negro musician, Graham Jackson, had played many times for the President at Warm Springs, the last time at Thanksgiving dinner the autumn before. This time Jackson played "Going Home," and "Nearer My God to Thee."

The coffin was carried aboard the funeral train for the journey, through the day and the night, back to Washington.

It was of course purely accidental but it was fitting too, that Roosevelt's life had come to its end in this remote little Georgia town. Warm Springs had so long and so well expressed the ceaseless fight which he had had to make to preserve first his life and later his vigor from the paralysis that, in a sudden, swift stroke, had seemed a decade and more before to have brought his career to a close before it had really begun.

As the train moved slowly through the night, passing by guards drawn up at each little station, the sound of men and women singing hymns along the railroad side came over and over to those who were moving northward with the body.

Washington that morning was bright with sunshine. I remember that the Plaza at Union Station seemed to have been washed improbably clean by the sparkling air. Many people were standing quietly at the station, and had been for many hours. The body was brought from the train and, encased in the bronze casket, it was put upon a small black caisson. Now there was a second procession, from Union Station to the White House. It wound along two miles of march, through the semislums of the station area and past the green parks surrounding the Capitol and then through the business streets and finally to the gates of the White House itself. The military bands intermittently raised their somber airs. But mostly there was a great silence broken only by the soft footfalls of marching servicemen and women and by sobs which could be heard in whispers as thin as the sound of falling leaves. There was a slight military display in this march, but the note of military power was the least insistent note in an unforgettable cavalcade. It was a pageant, yes; but the pageantry was largely unnoticed and unseen. The eye was caught and fixed—it seemed that every eye was caught and fixed—upon the black-covered coffin that lay upon the dark caisson. The people hardly had time to spare a glance even for Mrs. Roosevelt or for the new President of the United States, Mr. Harry Truman. Through Delaware Avenue and then down Constitution Avenue with all its heavy marble buildings and then past the old Treasury Building on Fifteenth Street and then leftward into Pennsylvania Avenue and then at last to the White House—so wound the procession. The bands played "Onward Christian Soldiers" and then "Adeste Fideles" and then, again and again, came the heavy beat of "The Dead March" from *Saul* and the measured heartbreak of Chopin's "Funeral March." In all this scene of marines and sailors and soldiers and airmen and Wacs and Waves and Spars the caisson itself seemed oddly small as so gently it trundled along.

Indeed, the black rectangular and tiny object that was the caisson stood out, amid the movement and spectacle that surrounded it, as the core of all this movement and the core of all the thoughts of the watching men and women that morning. It was like a small, dark jewel displayed alone in a vast, lighted window, drawing and compelling all eyes, centering itself in the memories and in the forebodings and hopes of all minds. It was the inwardness of the scene, the sense of the going home of the scene, which one felt then and which most of all one remembers now. This had been a man of many paradoxes; and paradox was perhaps the deepest of all the symbols that moved along beside this procession of death. That body there had represented, in itself alone while it had remained live and quick, the greatest concentration of power ever to reside in any President of this country; in any leader of *any* country devoted to the ordered supremacy of the popular will. In that body there had been, only hours before, the ultimate source of command for ten millions of Americans who had been drawn into the military service of the United States. (And it had been, too, very close to the ultimate source of command for many more millions—British, French, Canadian, Australian, New Zealanders, Poles among them.)

The well-remembered "greetings" from this man via the draft board had sent the millions, the wealthy, the poor, the able, the foolish, the long, the short and the tall, around the world to military glory, to military tedium, to mud and jungle and sea and plain, to Arctic shore and desert sand, to death and sickness, to heartbreak and to a memorable richness of trial and success. That man had put the United States of America intimately and forever into the world, into every corner of it, from Eisenhower Platz in London (otherwise Grosvenor Square) to Guadalcanal, to the Coral Sea and to all the other far and incredible places about an earth that would never again be unfamiliar to our generation.

At least some of us who stood and watched that morning and listened to the mourning bands and unconsciously sought to settle our feet to the cadence of the funeral march were remembering the English Channel on the night before D Day, the smoke of liberated Manila and many other things and scenes from afar. But always the eye returned to the caisson in this small, homely street in Washington; always the mind

returned to dwell in sorrow and in weariness upon this procession which was two hours by the clock, but which was
endlessly spun out, too, to the length of half a lifetime. All
the world was here in this familiar street; but all the world
was thrust back far away. High endeavor was coming to the
end that morning not alone for the man who now lay dead
upon the caisson; high endeavor was ending also for the
thousands who watched directly, for the millions who listened
on the radio for the progress of the cavalcade across the
warm asphalt that had not been repaired too lately. (Why
those ugly potholes there in front of the gray and solid
Treasury? *Don't you know there's a war on, Mac?*)

But the very munificence of the vanished power that had
rested in the broken man we were bringing home upon the
caisson made its scope difficult to grasp; we should not soon
truly sense its absence. It was not the body of a great commander, of a great Magistrate, or even of a great politician
that was being drawn through the streets. It was the body
of a man who had somehow, and sometimes brusquely and
even arrogantly and with more than a touch of a cheerful
cynicism, made Americans all a part of each other—happily
or reluctantly and angrily each inescapably a part of the
other, so that thereafter our diversity, our pluralism, would
never again be what it had been when he came upon our
scene. It was the body of a man who had leveled downward
all those people and all those forces in our society who had
been either too powerful or simply too free and gay for the
new age, into an age of a "togetherness" long antedating the
adoption of that term as an advertising slogan. It was the body
of a man who had leveled upward all those people and those
forces who had been too oppressed (and also in many cases
too incompetent) to take important places in what was to become infinitely the greatest corporate merger ever carried

through in the United States—and a merger against which no possible antitrust law could ever have operated. This was the merger of the States into the Amalgamated (not quite the United) States of America, and the merger of the people into the Amalgamated People of the United States.

It was the body of a man who had for the first time in history in this hemisphere raised up a truly federated country; who had repealed, by the simple sanctions of a political force based upon vast and essentially inchoate political majorities, much of the reality (as distinguished from the literal Articles) of the Constitution of the United States. The very best part of that Constitution, the Bill of Rights, he had undeniably strengthened and infused with a new and deeper meaningfulness. But some other parts of the Constitution (not the *best* parts but valid parts and parts which history may yet show not to have been so casually expendable as he had thought) had been ended forever by partial nullification. The rights of the states which had been reserved by the Constitution for a century and a half had in fact, though not in form, been largely atrophied in his long term. This was no longer really a Union of the States whose people were gazing out that morning at a sad procession to the White House gates. The Union of the States which Lincoln had so hardly preserved had now been transformed, forever, by this man now dead, into a Union of the People. And this had been done by the most gifted, the most daring, and at heart one of the least sensitive politicians in our history, by the creation of transient and in some cases quite improbable majorities which he had made with an extraordinary mixture of practical idealism and naked opportunism.

It could fairly be said of him that on the whole he had proceeded in honest candor and not in stealth in this amazing, often gallant and sometimes brutal, peripheral assault upon what some had regarded as the greatest charter of government since Magna Charta. But assaulted it he had. And the terrible hostage to fortune he had left lay in the fact that what he had created could not, because of his own inevitable mortality, be carried forward in coherence and in strength after he had gone. The wisdom, the rightness, the competence of all wrenching reforms may rightly be endlessly debated. Unarguably, however, the creator of *any* reform owes an overriding, a decisive, responsibility to that reform, and to history, not to make a machine that cannot run in his absence or be controlled upon his departure from the scene.

Chapter

Thirteen

From the moment he had come to power in 1933—in a time so dark and foreboding that any sensible man had to accept the force of the argument that almost any experimentation was preferable to simply more of the gray and grisly drift of paralysis—Roosevelt had challenged the doctrine of States' Rights. Everything he had done in the field of economics had in fact—and properly so, in the sense that Expediency must at last confront Emergency—driven a dagger into this doctrine. For he had known, and in this he was right, that one could not restore a country to economic health and vigor so long as any state or any set of states retained the power to interpose actions against the common economic program of revival and survival. Depression never heard of a state line; Depression could not read the Constitution. One by one, the famous alphabetical agencies had been drawn up to take from the states their historic power to have some real control over the commerce within them. The true contest for years had not been, as Roosevelt had so often pictured it, a contest simply between the greedy rich and the misused poor, though both the greedy rich and the misused poor were surely and deeply involved in it in human terms. The true contest had been over the central issue whether the federal government for "good" purposes (and I for one thought them to be just that) could amend the Constitution to reduce not merely the

mercantile powers of the states but also their heretofore un-
challengeable basic position as the assigned repositories of
all such powers as had not been specifically granted to the
federal authority.

Lincoln's own funeral procession to Illinois of nearly a
century before was in the minds of many of us on that morning in Washington when Roosevelt was for the last time
coming home to the White House. Lincoln in his time had
altered the Constitution—or say, if you will, that he had added
a section on secession which had not theretofore really been
a visible part of the printed document—by federal bayonets.
(I have said before that I am a Southerner; or, if you prefer,
I have *admitted* that infamous personal condition and have
withheld any apology for it. I am not, however, anti-Lincoln,
nor do I really believe it would have been a good thing had
the South been allowed to break away and so to form another,
competing nation here.) What Lincoln had done with federal bayonets Roosevelt had done with the most fluid and
intuitively brilliant political leadership we had ever seen. All
the same, he had done it; he had amended the Constitution
without going through those dusty forms which had been
provided for such alterations. And in doing this, he had sometimes departed from what some of us, even now, still believe
in, the fair statement of the issue by its protagonists. One
could not, perhaps, expect the throat-clutching fairness of
the Lincoln-Douglas debates, which one will read and read
again in vain to find a single spurious or self-serving summary
by either debater or what his antagonist had said before him.

For though Roosevelt had been decently open as to what
he had been about, he had surely been less than open and
ingenuous in his methods for reaching his goal. In his campaign to put to death the rights of the states he had opened
the national dialogue—and so maintained it to the end—in such

a way as to oversimplify a grave question almost beyond belief. States' Rights were presented by him and by his people as only the "rights" to deny, rather than to protect and fulfill, the decent opportunities of the people. The quick political mind of the Roosevelt movement had instantly sensed the *seeming* intellectual untenability of a system of deliberately divided government. The quick, and sometimes not too fastidious, political shorthand of that movement had exploited, all too ably and well, the natural popular instinct against what were pictured, for illustrations, as the state "right" of Georgia to operate a chain gang for prisoners and the "right" of the Southern states in general to move in various ways to deny equal civil rights to the Negroes. All this was not only unfair, it was—worse yet—an almost ridiculous, and a very punishing, oversimplification of a Constitutional crisis of historic meaning and of historic dignity.

The fact that the system of jury trial is open to manifest abuse is one thing; the fact that popular elections are undoubtedly open to the corruptions of demagoguery is one thing. But these inherent vulnerabilities and disabilities do not, to men able to think, destroy the unique usefulness and rightness of the institutions of jury trial and popular elections. So with "states' rights." As an operating politician FDR was both sound in expediency and justified in ethics in moving pragmatically to qualify those rights in their application to a continentalized industrial and agrarian society that had become unavoidably national in its meaning and functioning. To accept all this as the reality of the Thirties and Forties and to proceed against it *with care not to go too far* had been Roosevelt's great opportunity. But, impatient and not excessively well-read or overly burdened with the truths of history, he had set out to destroy not simply what was no longer good and useful in the concept of States' Rights but also what had to be maintained unless we proposed, in plain truth, to alter the whole form of the American government.

For the profound attrition which Roosevelt had directed upon States' Rights—upon the good States' Rights as well as against the no-longer-good or -relevant ones—had led to the effective dissolution of state responsibilities in human areas that were of the most capital significance to the proper maintenance of the federal Republic itself. On the day he died every state still had the Constitutional obligation to sustain its own internal order, to educate its children, to make provision against such common dangers and problems as were not national in scope or external in origin.

But no state had any longer either the will so to do or, in terms of reality as distinguished from theory, even the political power so to do. The Roosevelt Revolution had not only largely broken up the ancient local political machines, like Tammany Hall in New York; it had also effectively deprived both local and state-wide politicians everywhere of the means to give true leadership to their people. The golden rush of federal grants-in-aid to the states which Roosevelt had initiated, while he was wisely and with profoundly good effect initiating the people generally into a real and continuing participation in the affairs of the federal government, had largely ended the capacity of the states to use either the carrot or the stick to bring their people forward alike into their opportunities and their responsibilities.

Effective and long-enduring political power in a democratic system, as in any political-party instrumentality, rests most of all upon the ability of the leaders to give things to the people—roads, schools, political jobs and all the rest—as well as to demand things of the people. The state and local politicians were first left without real patronage to hand out. Thus they were left without real disciplinary power. Next, the states themselves found their problems preempted by Washington, along with their power, and the solutions for those problems lodged now in the White House and not in the governors' mansions or the state legislatures. Thus, having been left without the power to discipline their party people, they were now left without the power to give things to their people.

And the essential drive which Roosevelt had made legislatively and administratively against state power had been accompanied, if in a spasmodic course that he himself sometimes described as one of "zigs and zags," by a drive against the inherent right of the states to be *different*. The ill-fated Roosevelt "purge" campaign of 1938, against Senators and Congressmen who either really were too non-Rooseveltian or simply were thought by him to be so, was only the most overt instance of this second finger of the pincers operation.

In all this, parenthetically, there lay abundant proof, to those who would seriously look at it, that Roosevelt had been always a domestic and not a world-viewing politician. For the crimes of the appointed purgees of 1938—Senators Millard Tydings in Maryland and Walter George in Georgia notable among them—had been wholly economic, which is to say, local and almost solely and merely mercantile crimes. However regrettably out of step they might have been thought to have been in such matters as labor reform and minimum wages, they were absolutely indispensable men to the far higher designs to which Roosevelt had been reluctantly and at last forced to turn his attention in the world of an emergent and triumphant fascism. It was George of Georgia (along with another less than total Roosevelt man named Tom Connally of Texas) who had supplied the essential leadership for repealing the arms embargo, for bringing forward lend-lease, for putting the United States, in short, in position to do its simple duty to a world in torture. And a long time after this Roosevelt funeral procession had moved so somberly through Washington's streets, it was to be Tydings of Maryland who would put his political life to the test (and lose it) in taking the lead to defend the memory of the Roosevelt Administration and the integrity of the then current Truman Administration from the twentieth-century know-nothingism of the McCarthyites of the Fifties. If States'-Rightsism as opposed to total Roosevelt federalism had not prevailed in 1938 in the cotton patches of Georgia (chain gangs nonetheless) and in the strangely mixed urban-rural life of Maryland, the sadness of this day of Roosevelt's last home-coming to Washington would have been no less keen, to be sure. But one States'-Righter, George, had already well and even nobly served the man who, lying dead now, had once tried to destroy him. And the other States'-Righter, Tydings, was soon to serve, too, against an effort to slander not simply Roosevelt but much for which he had stood so long.

No one, I least of all, can now pretend that he had a private view of the future on that sunny morning of Saturday, April 14, 1945, when the funeral train pulled into Washington with muffled bell and muted whistle. But, looking back now in time upon that moment of the long-ago April, one may perhaps even suggest this:

The wreckage of state power which lay symbolically around Roosevelt's funeral cortege, as one of the least desir-able of the great, strange medley of bequests he had left, was long to be with us. It was long to impede the right progress of the nation which in many ways he had left so strongly and surely standing. Is it not possible that the tragic failure of the Southern states to make in time a reasonable accom-modation of the race issue, particularly in its impact on public education, could have sprung in part from the destruction of both the power and the sense of responsibility of the states? Is it not possible, at least, that states full of a sense of their duty, rather than stripped of their sense of governmental mission, might, in the new airs of tolerance and compassion and oneness that blew across the world with the defeat of fascism, have found the means for offering something better than separate-but-equal education, as the Supreme Court was long afterward to be compelled to order them to do?

Even as one asks the question he concedes that the Southern states had in fact gone through many decades before without making or seriously attempting such reforms.

Still, there is surely something to be said for the fact that the war had now brought a new world and a new climate; that it had mixed and mingled Southern Americans as well as Northern Americans with men of many races and creeds and religions all about the world; and that it had taught these Americans—the Southerners as well as the Northerners—that the "colored" of this earth knew equally with the white how to fight in faith and honor, how to die for comrades with that quiet, ultimate loyalty which proves the true ultimate brotherhood in decency of all humankind.

And one must also always remember this: Roosevelt had never once made his assault on States' Rights into a determined assault on such equivocal States' "Rights" as the "right" to proceed unfairly, in either voting or in employment, against minority groups.

True it was that on this day of his funeral procession the special sorrow of the Negroes ran like a dark, manifest thread through the streets of Washington; no deeper mourners had he than these. But their veneration of him rested—whether in every case they knew it or not—not as on a Lincoln who had spiritually emancipated them. FDR's concern had been for their right to eat, not their right to a full political freedom.

He had taken no effective step directly to forward their general voting rights. His executive orders against racial discriminations had been, in plain truth, far fuller of rhetoric than of resolution. (Truman would attempt more; Eisenhower still more; and Kennedy far more, in this field.)

It could fairly be said that what Roosevelt had given the Negroes was not full political justice, but rather a fuller dinner pail; he had lifted their spirits, just as he had lifted the spirits of all other Americans. (His wife, Eleanor, had tried to do much more than this by personal example; but there is no evidence whatever that the President himself ever looked with much favor upon Mrs. Roosevelt's exertions in this area.)

One could say of Lincoln that when he fought a Civil War against an old, excessive concept of States' Rights he fought it for grand objectives. But Roosevelt's campaign against States' Rights had in it none of this flavor of a high evangelism. He had set out against States' Rights—the good along with the bad—for no higher motive than to improve the country's industrial-labor strength. It is not that this was an ignoble motive. It is simply that the great resultant loss of our old unique pluralism, of the many separate public authorities operating under the ultimate headship of the one federal authority, was a rather high price to pay for a purpose which was not so lofty as preserving a great Union but only so mundane as making the wheels of commerce turn faster and more fruitfully.

Chapter

Fourteen

It is, I think, at least an arguable proposition. But we were not looking out, on that day, upon what might have been. We were looking instead, so many of us in still and painful grief, on what had been and upon a man who had been and was now no more. Think, then, of Harry Truman, riding gravely and unnoticed in that funeral parade, as he confronted in his mind what had been left to him to do, to try to do—and never in the world to be able to do at all.

He had been left abruptly in charge of a Democratic Party he never made; of an Administration he never had a chance to understand; of a country which in the space of the twelve years of Franklin D. Roosevelt's leadership had changed more basically, and in more ways, than it ever before had changed in any period of half a century.

We had come through much darkness, the darkness of economic catastrophe, the darkness of great war. But we had, all the same, not come out upon a plateau of light, or even of peace. The historic and successful challenger of economic want (and one repeats and repeats this feat as Roosevelt's supreme and unexampled gift to his people) had nevertheless actually fostered rather than ended an excessive materialism which so far as the eye of speculation could reach would remain an unpleasant stain upon the national character. I, for one, do not quarrel overmuch with this. One must recognize that just as total external war must be paid for in dreadful coin, even in victory, so must war against economic injustice at home be paid for in coin that will be sometimes ugly.

To be sure, the New Materialism of the masses that had been left by Roosevelt was, in the ethical sense, less objectionable than had been the old Materialism of the Favored which he had forever destroyed. There had been a permanent defeat of truly large-scale American hunger and of truly large-scale American unemployment. Over these Roosevelt had indeed won, for good, through the federal mechanisms which he had set up—to the howling horror of the ultra-conservatives of the Thirties who were to become the moderates and even the "modern Republicans" of the late Fifties and early Sixties who would universally support bank-deposit insurance and most of all the rest. But if he had mastered the "economic royalists," as surely he had done, this comparative handful of selfish and often vapid men were to be succeeded by nearly a whole nation of economic gluttons. And who—with a selfishness no less than that of the Liberty Leaguers who had so melodramatically engaged Roosevelt in the Thirties like fat elderly Home Guardists shooting Springfield rifles at paratroopers armed with Tommy-guns—would soon stand at the forefront of these unlovely characters? Well, the lean and devoted and hungry labor philosophers of the Thirties were to become the obesely arrogant and overprivileged labor bosses of two decades later. The distracted farmers of the Thirties had seen their whole *raison d'être* destroyed by lost markets, overdue mortgages and the terrible erosions of both soil and spirit. All this they had bravely borne—though it is true that on occasion their agonies had become insupportable and here and there they had taken up their shotguns to meet the sheriff's men in barn or field or woodlot. But these farmers, in so many instances, were to become the greedily distended and flabby swallowers of endlessly overdone federal subsidies, elderly cry-babies who were to forget the deep honor of their estate as the indispensable growers of the elemental things their fellow men must have to eat and to wear. Put the corn in the federal bin; float the cotton down the river; *they* didn't give a damn. They were to join that vast American phalanx —almost, truth to tell, that American majority—which, as the saying was to go, "didn't give a damn." The store clerks who didn't give a damn, either for the boss or the customer. The carpenters who didn't give a damn whether the plank was truly or crookedly nailed up. The "relief clients" so ready to accept a status which, while in no sense indecent, had once been regarded as acceptable only in utter personal extremity when absolutely no work of any kind was to be had. The ex-"war worker" who, having seduced the wife of the fifty-dollar-a-month soldier in beer-tavern overtures, would soon be "looking around for another job," and taking his time about it—while he cheerfully defrauded his late employer, the government, on his income tax.

What was opening out before us, in that morning of a majestically unsordid national grief, was the unloveliest period, in terms of manners, if not of morals, and in terms of irresponsibility if not of worse, that this nation had ever known. All of us could remember, and most of us could remember with resentment, the litany of warning and protest with which for endless years the anti-Rooseveltians had bored to distraction the very air itself: The man who had never met a payroll was ruining the United States; he was killing free enterprise; he was destroying the instinct for competition; he was regimenting and cheapening the whole American society; he was ending the power of management to manage and the willingness of worker to work; he was sapping the vital strength of capitalism; and so on, and so on.

It was mostly nonsense when it had been said. And even in the time to come men looking at it fairly would not be able to say that this man now dead had really done all these destructive things to the spirit of the country he had loved. But in that same time to come it could be fairly said that there was a chemical trace of truth in these long caveats. For, in plain fact, the man who had taken so very much responsibility to himself alone *had* reduced the power of his people to accept and to face their own private and group responsibilities.

In his lifetime the national discussion about Roosevelt had been either-or; either he was the greatest man who had ever lived, or he was the worst scoundrel ever sent to the White House by a bemused and misbegotten electorate. Now that he lay dead in honorable exhaustion the very fact of his death tended somewhat to mute, among all but the most bitter, the harshest of that sleepless animus that had for fourteen years filled the days and nights of those who had hated him. But in his death the grief of his idolators was already, on this very morning of the funeral procession to the White House, hardening into the murky emotionalism of those who mourn not a man but a martyr. It was not soon to be possible to speak of this man, this man of so much ability and also of so much blindness, in measured and adult tones without being reviled by the "eithers" or by the "ors."

All the same, emotion is not history; it is mind, not heart, that must in the end prevail in any judgment suitable to and creditable to mature and civilized men. Thus it would be said in retrospect that while war and all sorts of other external factors had had a great and perhaps even a decisive part in it, Roosevelt on that morning of his last return to the White House was leaving a country whose objective place in the world was far higher than the world's subjective estimate of it could possibly have allowed.

For among the great facts of the American past which were receding that day into memory was the old fact that this has been, but would be no more, a country of *manners* as well as of mines and manufactures. Somehow as we had become more secure economically—in our businesses, in our farms, in our jobs—we had become in some deep and largely inexplicable way more crude, more selfish and less truly compassionate than we had been before. Everybody, everywhere, had begun wildly to overstate his own rights and privileges, and profoundly to understate his own obligations and responsibilities.

To some of those who look upon life as a mural made up alike of opportunity and of duty one of the great, unuttered issues as Roosevelt had moved with a sure skill to strengthen the country and its people materially had been this: Would his noble, if essentially limited, purposes not entail infinitely less worthy consequences as well? These observers, not being mere childish reactors to the automatic slogans of Roosevelt's automatic opposition, had not been at all concerned that he had "never met a payroll." They had not been concerned with his alleged lack of expertise in the myths and thin social values of the "businessman" community which, before him, had ruled this country with tasteless plan and for tasteless objectives.

They had been concerned, instead, that FDR's understandable urgency in repairing the economic destructions of the Depression might end in the undue elevation of that new concept called man's "economic rights," to the hurt and depreciation of man's ancient duties as a creature charged to live his life for more than bread alone. They had feared, in short, for the American *style*, while they fully acknowledged the bitter and biting first necessity for restoring the American capacity to work and the American opportunity to eat and to prosper in a larger economic society.

No more exquisitely balanced human problem had ever been confronted by a politician. When a leader must do two things that have in them some aspect of mutual exclusiveness he must, of course, do first the thing that more urgently needs to be done. He must then hope that in accomplishing this priority he may somehow reach, at least, part of the way toward the lesser, if still important, and second priority. In this case the second problem, the preservation and expansion of the good American style, had been greatly neglected. In no way had it been met. Many an emotionally honest man, many a man of intellectual integrity, has looked down upon the body of a fallen loved one with a sorrow not less genuine for a simultaneous awareness that the fallen one has left this earth in some ways worse, as well as in other ways better, for his having been here.

So it was that one mourner, at any rate—the mourner who here raises this unapologetically mixed salute to Franklin Delano Roosevelt—looked down that morning upon the caisson as so slowly, almost so tenderly, it moved along with the body of a great man who had saved so many people from so much; who had left so many people so much richer and so much poorer all at once. The time of Franklin Roosevelt was ending in the death not only of this great man—and a truly irreplaceable man, he was—but in the death also of certain American attitudes that were, one felt then and feels now, not themselves expendable, either. Not the least of our old glories had been the glory of our diversity in this vast continental redoubt of individualism where once the right to be wrong and wrongheaded and uncooperative and cussed had been a right beyond prize.

Not the least of those old glories had been the instinctive willingness of the people to honor privacy—privacy in one's self; privacy in one's work; privacy, if one chose, in pursuing one's private error. Not the least of those old glories had been the right to be polite and even deferential without being thought to be weak; the right to be scrupulous in giving value for value received without being thought to be a toady or a "scab." There had been, before, many mansions in the great house of American life. Now, all the rooms had been thrown together into one vast room where there was far more common security but where far fewer dreams were dreamed; where there was far more common strength but far fewer strong, separate men; where there was far more social justice but far fewer instances of social excellence; where there was far more "mutual tolerance"—a pompous and meaching phrase, that!—but far less kindness for kindness's sake.

The great, mixed, atonal murmur of the American speech had become homogenized into a sharper, a shriller, medley. And there was in this medley a good deal more of the note of a self-demanding snarl than we had known in the long ago. "Thank you" was now a term less and less used. Certain intangible gifts, the gift of mere courtesy, the gift of mere mannerliness from merchant to buyer and from buyer to merchant, from employer to employee and from employee to employer, were not now so much exchanged as once they had been. The palpable coin in our purses had surely greatly increased. And he, the man lying in the coffin on the caisson, had had much to do with making this so. But had he also caused those other things, the debased coin of courtesy, the end of mannerliness? Those fleeting, those endless, hours of the funeral procession, were neither short enough nor long enough to answer exactly and clearly these questions in a man's mind. Nor have been all the hours that have since spun

out in time. But it is possible to make the beginning of an
approach to an answer: Not even Roosevelt had held in his
hands alone all the world and all the changes in that world
that had come in his time. War itself had been both destructive of and immensely enriching to the American spirit, a
quality that may be defined, in this context, neither as high
spiritualism nor as mere concern about correctness in conduct.
What is meant instead is a kind of illumined *élan* with which
to confront both life itself and all those other men who pass
through it along with oneself. For this had been made a better
country in one way on that very morning of the procession
of death by all those who, in the accidents of fate, had been
involved in war's cutting edge, involved in combat.

Men all along the world's firing lines had learned a compassion, a brotherhood washed clean of all mawkishness, free of
all spurious "tolerance" and catchpoll demagoguery. What
they had learned would work a bit against, though never stay,
the tide of material selfishness, the cheap, secondhand, second-
grade cynicism of puerility which was to run through our
country for many years to come. In the shorthand view of history, at least, Roosevelt had sent these men to the far places
where they had learned what they had learned. So in this small
and tenuous sense he could be said to have promoted a right
élan. But in much larger senses he was leaving a country less,
rather than more, informed of man's true brotherhood. Mer-
cantilism he had honorably saved. "Better living standards" he
had decently made. But the great bulk of the people had surely
learned during the time of his leadership—though not through
his intention or purposes—a vulgar and wholly overempha-
sized new love of Number One, a precious self-petting
attitude, a whining self-aggrandizement and crude personal
selfishness which was quite mistakenly regarded as only a
heightened self-respect. To confront upon their return this

new American character was not the least of those hard problems of "readjustment to civilian life" upon which many ex-fighting men were to be hopelessly broken and toward which many others would have to make an unendingly uneasy peace of necessity.

It would be said many times of Roosevelt that in saving the country's life he had lost its soul. This, of course, was melodramatic exaggeration. All the same there would be enough truth in it, as time went on, to suggest that a peculiar weakness of crudity had entered the American character to a degree not seen in other countries which had also been engaged in hostilities. We were entering, that very morning of the procession, an era in which the more we had the less we were willing honorably to earn it; in which the word *possession* was to become the most profound word in the American language.

Those who had so lately had far too little were now not only to have far too much but also to put an inflated value on what they did have. And they were to aspire mainly only to those things which in a truly civilized society are regarded as comparatively valueless. The two cars in every garage, the chicken in every pot, which the bewildered and unhappy Herbert Hoover had once promised—these and much more were now to be had easily on every hand. Wealth accumulated, for a certainty. And if they did not actually decay, men surely lost much that once was irreplaceable in our national life. And they seemed so little to regret that which was lost.

Decent workmanship, what might be called the integrity of honestly *trying*, declined sadly and in every part of the society. The old Republican cry that FDR was raising up a people solely interested in "handouts from Washington" had not been true when first the slogan was coined; and it was never to be seen to be true. For the new special dependence of the people, the new and undue dependence of the people, was not so simply based and could never be so simply stated.

Some would say that it was a dependence based upon the determination to have "something for nothing." But this too was a case of special pleading, directed not really at the people but at Roosevelt himself. This was a mere harsh partisan rationale and rallying cry not intended to assist (or even to interpret) a country but only to help win this or that election.

In a sense, Roosevelt's time had left still forming a peculiarly clear-cut patch among all the patches that are in the mosaic of style and manner which is a part of our national history. We had opened our nationhood some two centuries before in a triumph for the materialism of parsimony, the grudging grabbing for the glory of the Lord, of Puritan New England. The Puritans had set this early national style after an easy contest for dominance of manners over the charming, feckless, richer, more sophisticated, and perhaps unduly light-minded tidewater English colonists in Virginia and the Carolinas to the South.

But materialism in this early era had marched alongside a harsh sense of private duty and a conviction that earning things by hard work was good for the soul. This sort of view had on the whole prevailed from the founding of the federated Republic to the close of the War Between the States in which, again, the manner of the gay and idle types, the Southerners, was overcome finally and forever.

Then the Reconstruction had followed the death of a President (Lincoln) very similar to Roosevelt in his overmastering care for the people rather than for the stability of the national style. A degradingly excessive materialism had characterized that period; it was as though the people were in a fever of revulsion from the idealism, if practical idealism, of Abraham Lincoln. This, however, was a materialism of robber barons and of high thieves and economic bandits. And this, again, was a time when, on the whole, private responsibility was still held to be an unavoidable private obligation. The vast majority of the people still earned a great deal more than they got.

What was now to open upon us, after Roosevelt in point of time if not necessarily because of a revulsion similar to that which had followed the death of Lincoln, was a new kind of materialism.

It was to be a frantic grasping not by a few railroad and oil and meat-packer trust-raisers. It was to be a frantic grasping by nearly a whole people. It was to be a period in which never had so many unworthy material ambitions been realized by so many whose private consciences were to become lost in a new collective social conscience which they were so to pervert and to oversimplify as to shame the man who had been its activator. This man whose body now rested on the caisson, Franklin Roosevelt, had died to make a better economic order for the ordinary man. I recall thinking on that day of the funeral procession that it was as well, perhaps, that he had not lived to see how very ordinary this man was to become; had not lived to see in all its smallness and ugliness the progressive cheapening of his dream which even then could be sensed by any one lately returned to this land of the big creature comfort. Even in war the United States had grown so fat; so much like one vast PX where it was all on the house.

Wherein had he failed—if failed he had, indeed—in leaving all this, too, as a part of his multisided legacy to his country? Had he, himself, toward the end of his life been uneasily and faintly aware that one of the four freedoms he had done so much to redeem—freedom from want—was becoming to so many also a freedom from adult responsibility, and from taste? Some I know who well knew him think now that this is possible. If so, it was not the first time that a leader had carried indispensable reform too far forward too fast at the expense of traditional values. When the ship is tossing in a great storm many things not immediately required in the savage contest between captain and sea may fall overboard in the darkness and confusion. Is it the captain's blame? Or is it the sea's?

This captain, who had practiced the inspired higher selfishness which regards first and foremost the interests of the many, had himself been very clear about what he was doing and why. He had, however—as any real politician must often actually do—made the tactic of oversimplification actually a *public policy* in order to be able to deal at all with matters that were conditions and not theories. Management had become far too strong; labor, until he had come upon the scene fourteen years before this procession of death in the streets of Washington, had become far too weak.

All across the economic landscape there had been an imbalance that was wrong in principle and also wrong in the purely practical sense. Too few had far too much economic power; too many had far too little. So, sometimes rather like a kindly avuncular storyteller on a garrulous visit to his poorer relations, Roosevelt had set up before the people a series of neat black-and-white tableaux between type figures presented as The Rich and The Poor, The Privileged and The Underprivileged. He would master the former in behalf of the latter. And so, too, to a considerable extent he had done.

It had been a perfectly right and proper thing to do. But he had not reckoned upon one human fact of life: To be rich and oppressive is surely to practice a cold vice. But the poor and the oppressed are not therefore, necessarily and in themselves, the sole representatives of virtue. Those for whom times have been altogether too hard are not incapable, once the scheme of things has been changed, of demanding that times be made altogether too soft for them. The reforms that Roosevelt had made stood in their rightful dignity now that he was gone. But a leader in making his reforms is required to take measures against their less desirable, as well as to forward their undoubtedly desirable, probable consequences.

To some who looked on that morning while the bands raised their mournful brass and fell silent and then mourned again and fell silent, gloomy thoughts of these less desirable consequences were part of all the medley of sound and sight and impression that entered the mind and heart. As this lusty, cheerful, largehearted man was being carried along now in death, this was another of the father images that shimmered before one's consciousness: This patriarch of the nation, like many a father of a family, had done too much, sometimes, for its welfare; and too little to make it learn to stand alone. He had given the nation's people much. But one gift he had not given, or had not been able to give. He had not strengthened them to use rightly all that he had given them.

He had been a very human man, lacking the chill and almost exclusively intellectual perceptions of the last Democratic President before him, Woodrow Wilson. And, very human though he was, he had lacked also the tactile gut understanding of the common man which was so much a part of the successor who now sat so gravely—and so unnoticed— in the slowly moving automobile in the somber parade which was bearing Franklin Roosevelt to the White House for a funeral service and Harry Truman to the White House for what were to be hard and bitter and memorable years in the long story of the Presidency.

For Truman knew for a fact that the common man's qualities were not solely those qualities which Lincoln had once suggested that God must have loved so very much. Truman knew because he knew common men. To Roosevelt, love for the common man had been wholly genuine; but actually it had been a secondhand and an uninformed love. Roosevelt had loved common man in the abstract and in the mass. He had not *known* common man; nor had common man in the singular and literal sense ever been close to him at any point in his life in anything he had done. Indeed, there had been an almost touching and naïve generosity in him which did not sense the selfishness as well as the courage and decency of ordinary people. All his life this man had thought of "the people"—but all his life he had actually dealt with only special kinds of people. He had a rarely comparable knowledge of the ways and the weaknesses of powerful people; he merely idealized (though never sentimentalized) the ordinary people. It was this idealization of attitude, quite as much as the policies he had followed, which had so infuriated those old boys in the old clubs who had long and so bitterly muttered that Franklin was a traitor to his class. Surely, they didn't understand common man either; but they didn't care about common man, and they thought he did not, either.

Nothing in the life that had now ended had prepared Roosevelt to understand the masses of the people. Not the least of the many ironies of his Administration had been the almost universal assumption that he did. What he had understood was not the masses but rather what moved them; he knew what they needed; he never knew what they were. It was this seeming lack which most of all proved the authentic genius of his leadership. For political genius is far more often found in this kind of awareness than in the kind of awareness that simply apprehends men. He knew the whole profound rhythm of the tides, the vast, deep moving forces among men. The other kind of leader knows only how ordinary man responds; Roosevelt knew what made him respond.

Only two kinds of men *really* know common man. One is common man himself; the other is the aristocrat. The upper-middle class, of which this dead President had been so distinguished a representative, is closer to common man in the purely structural sense in such faint vestiges as survive of the vertical class system. But in the true human sense the upper-middle-class man is farther from common man; it is a longer way to the bottom from the upper middle of the pile than it is from the very top.

All the same, common man in this country had never known such a sense of loss as it knew on this day—never known it even on that day nearly a century before when Lincoln fell. For, to repeat, Roosevelt had been truly a President of the people, meaning a distinct majority of them, whereas Lincoln had been the President of a majority of a part of the people.

Chapter

Fifteen

And what was being left this day was a people conditioned by Roosevelt to a new kind of Republic, which the popular will had permitted him fundamentally to alter, in its whole basic mechanism. In his life, the Constitution's system of checks and balances had a thousand times been flung in an admonitory way against him. He had been charged with having ignored the checks (those, that is, specifically on the power of the Presidency) and with having largely ignored the general balances, that delicately poised triune set of coequal powers—Executive, Legislative, Judicial—which had been laid down by the Founders.

Now that he was dead we were going to see that there was more truth in this charge than there had been temperateness in the way it had been leveled by his enemies. And it was going to look to be a more serious charge in the United States of the post-Roosevelt years than it could possibly have looked while he remained upon the scene. For while he was still here the imbalance of Constitutional powers within the government which he had created had seemed at worst only a theoretical thing—and, as a practical matter, only a debating point. He had believed most of all in making the great engine of government work. Like old Andy Jackson so long before him, he had wanted first to get good things done and to discuss later, if at all, precisely how they were done.

No one but a frantic partisan had need, while he was alive, really to worry too much about all this. For the enormous power he had so gladly—and often gallantly—exercised had been based upon an ultimate sanction, that of the people, which is respectable in any language. All the same, both the implied mandate so to act beyond and apart from the Constitution, and above all the capability of successors so to act, had expired when his own life had drawn to its close. He had left a record of extra-Constitutional action, which, regardless of his intentions, had in deep spirit if not in actual text changed the operative meaning of the Constitution itself. Moreover, he had, though not by design, placed upon Harry Truman the impossible burden of carrying out a new concept of the powers of the Presidency which could never have been carried out except by the man who had, with his matchless gift for evoking public support, made that concept.

Great Presidents make great works—and great mischief, sometimes, for those who come after them. So it was with Roosevelt. His long, confused and bitter contest with the courts had left not merely Roosevelt himself but the Presidency as an institution in a position not exactly as master of the judicial branch but with a continuing power to challenge it, if need be repeatedly, as it never had been challenged before his time. Moreover, his heavy and ultimately successful pressure on the Supreme Court to alter its views on the relationship of the Constitution to economic matters—to consider the new bread-and-butter rights of such as union labor and subsidized farmers as well as the ancient and established rights of individual political freedom—had revolutionized American justice. The whole human tone and complexion and philosophy of the Court had changed radically in his time and was to change yet more in the future. This Court on the day of his death had become more the public's familiar, and less the august and heretofore remote guardian of what the Constitution had said were private rights. If more compassion had entered the Court, a certain degree of its old icy competence and unparalleled distinction had surely left it. If liberal men exulted, as they did, that the Court of the "Nine Old Men" was gone—that bench of immense conservatism and sometimes of actual reaction—the Court of the newer men could be called only a very qualified triumph for rational liberalism.

The Court had become more liberal on the legislative issues of Roosevelt's era—those measures of a modified collectivism which he had undertaken to end economic anarchy, as a physician may prescribe desperate remedies for the desperately ill. But it had become considerably less liberal with respect to certain of the old-fashioned rights. Undeniably, an open doctrinaire struggle had been set off by Roosevelt among its formerly glacially reserved black-robed men. And long was this struggle to run. For the first time in all history the word "unseemly" had begun to be applicable, on occasion, to this, the only truly lofty secular institution within the American society. Institutions which are touched with mysticism (and the Supreme Court alone among all our instrumentalities of government had for a century been so touched) are not wisely made more earthy—even for indisputably good reasons.

We had not had a monarchy in this country. All this we had rejected in the beginning; for, in theory at least, our great revolt had been from a king and from the kingly tradition. All the same, Western humanity deeply requires some of the things which Western humanity believes it rejects. So the Court itself had been made dynastic; its members to serve for life; its members not to be questioned save by the practically impossible process of impeachment by the Congress of the United States.

The single word "removed," meaning totally detached and operating from a separate plane as from afar, has always more than any other word connoted what we meant by justice, as it has always done in the parent British order. This is why we so carefully inquire into any mass bias that might be held by prospective jurors. This is why we so isolate the jury, once it is impaneled. This is why we do not really like the system of electing judges. Even in those states and communities where this is done, the common effort is still to "keep the judges out of politics."

Now, for the first time, the Supreme Court of the United States was not so removed; and never again would be or could be. For the intrusion on it by Franklin Roosevelt, the man now being returned to the White House in death, had been the first *open* intrusion of like character it ever had suffered from the White House. The intrusion, because of its nature—and, yes, even because of its candor—had forever ended the apartness of the Court. More than this, it had put the Court directly into politics; blandly, yes, carefully yes, but into politics all the same. (It is true that Andrew Jackson—again, this the rough frontiersman had had much in common with the squire from the Hudson River—had once dared the Court to enforce a ruling he did not like. But he had not gone from this to an effort actually to enlarge the Court's field of umpires in the very middle of the game.)

So the enduring meaning of Roosevelt's effort in the late Thirties to "pack" the Court by adding new members was to go infinitely beyond the fairly limited and measurable purposes which he had had in mind. His intention had been simply to overcome what he had regarded as certain reactionary tendencies, in economic matters, of one bench at one time in history. Indeed, the word "history" is perhaps too large a word. For FDR's sense of history had been neither deep nor overly respectful. The President now succeeding him, this gray "little man" Harry Truman, had actually read and understood a great deal more of history and actually held a far greater and more reverent perception of this curiously blended art-science which is the very blood stream of national life and the sole attribute of immortality in states and systems.

To Roosevelt, history was what a man like himself would make it. To Truman, history was what made men. To Roosevelt, history was a book or a series of books, perhaps dull, perhaps sprightly, which a busy man might or might not read or heed. It was the work of men who had *written* but not *acted;* it was, in a term that had become so familiar during the wartime, not of the highest priority, nor even of the second highest. This body now being drawn through the streets of Washington on the dark caisson represented all that remained of a man who had been a great activist but an indifferent thinker; a political *artist* who for his masterpieces took his materials wherever and however they might lie to hand; whose joy was in the doing. This was no Presidential scholar; this was not a "wise" President. This instead was a President of brilliant intuitions who had gladly left it to others learnedly to discuss the theoretical considerations which they had supposed had moved him—but which had in fact never moved him at all. It had been his habit always to come zestfully to grips with what *was* in this world; he had never sighed over what might have been—or even much over what ought to have been or why, except to the degree that he might change what ought to have been to what was.

The Constitution itself had been to him in many times of political and legislative crisis largely one of those theoretical considerations. No doubt it was a fine thing, no doubt it was even a noble thing. But it was, after all, a *document.* And, often in his view, it was a document which had more significance in that rather dim art-science he had never troubled much to grasp, history, than it had meaning to what he saw as the one vibrant reality, the here and now of the people's interests.

I remember thinking as I looked down upon this slowly moving cavalcade that morning that in the people's eyes there lay upon this caisson the unique Presidential Hero of our national experience. This was Hero Incarnate to them precisely because this tall, thick-shouldered, handsome and fearless man had *acted;* had shared their distrust for the intangible, the philosophical, for the maybe-yes, maybe-no. He had believed only in going forward and not in thinking backward even at those times when a wiser, if far less appealing, leader would have deemed it best to attach the present and the future, at many points, to the past. For him, time had begun afresh with every morning's sun; for him the task each morning had been cheerfully to smash the problem that lay before him, leaving it for the housekeeper—or somebody—to sweep up the resulting rubbish. These residues he had considered little more than he would have considered the endless cigarette butts that sometimes had overflowed onto his bedcovers and onto his billowing, mountainous pajamas when he had finished his gusty breakfasts in bed while polishing off the "Go slow" admonitions—whether of timidity or of tradition—which anxious official visitors would bring before him.

This man would, for example, have been the worst possible judge, even had his legal learning been far greater that it was. He never had concerned himself with the fine points of things. Indeed, he had not been concerned with certain Constitutional and legal points which to other and deeper, if less inventive, minds were far from being merely fine. He would, however, have been an incomparable soldier in the grand manner had the accidents of life turned him to a military career—a Yankee Jeb Stuart with a plume in his hat; a charger up the San Juan Hill of his generation, as his kinsman Theodore Roosevelt had been in his generation. He was what in the war had been called "the assault type of general," with all the cheerful bravery, the glad, robust derring-do, of that type, which never let the pale cast of thought overly obscure its vision of action and yet more action. Indeed, one of the images of Roosevelt that was, I think, uppermost in the consciousness of those who were attending this funeral parade was that of the lost, gallant captain who had now left the great company of the people in the command of an unknown lieutenant, Truman, who was not then—and never later—to stir the emotions as the Old Man had done. There was a deep, instinctive fitness in the fact that in this last of his many parades Roosevelt was being given the sort of farewell that is traditional for fighting men—the caisson, the heavy, martial hymns of the marching, the playing, bands.

It was, here again, a day of many sad ironies. For the bespectacled Lieutenant Truman, who never looked the part at all, had in fact been an actual assault soldier, while the departed chief who had so looked the part had never been at all. And the man who had gone had left his office, the Presidency, enriched at the expense of other institutional values which were themselves needed by the people far more than they had recognized in his time and far more than they were fully to apprehend ever again.

As he had left the Supreme Court more popular and more active but with less essential strength and dignity, and the Constitution more flexible but less uncompromised, so he had left the legislative power deeply shaken.

The First Hundred Days of the first Roosevelt New Deal had seen more than an unexampled Presidential effort to lift the nation from economic fear and actual want. And so had most of the years since. A House of Representatives had actually passed major "bills" which were, in fact, at the time of their passage only simulated by rolled-up newspapers held aloft by the floor leaders. There had not been time enough to consider the issues even to the extent of having those issues put on paper in recognizable parliamentary language and terms. Even the Senate of the United States, the storied home of fierce legislative independence from the White House, had many times been bent brusquely to the will of a man who in running a race with disaster had sometimes found the Constitution to be altogether too slow a companion for his purposes.

The Congress had more than once been called upon by this powerful, this insistent, President to approve legislation which the President himself quite frankly knew to be of exceedingly doubtful Constitutionality. Moreover, these had been for the most part legislative acts whose philosophy placed Roosevelt's "new economic freedom" well above the older and more fundamental freedoms in the hierarchy of national values.

In the world-wide economic distress of the Thirties this had been by no means a unique consequence of the exercise of emergency leadership in the Western countries. Nearly everywhere leaders had looked for remedies that would work and had not been too choosy of methods to make them work. In saving the right of private property Roosevelt had been required to use the enormous real, implied and arrogated powers of a singular office, that of the Presidency, to beat down the hesitations, proper as well as improper, of a collective office known as the Congress. And in saving this right of private property he had been required repeatedly to wound it, much as a surgeon may remove an arm to rescue a life. It had been the *nature* of this surgical operation that had deeply troubled the true and civilized conservatives.

But it had been the *mere fact* of this surgical operation that had thrown into transports of rage the ultraconservatives, who were, on this very day of national mourning, uttering blasphemously relieved farewells to the dead President for whom so many others were weeping, in their eyes or in their hearts. Sophisticated men spoke then—and have spoken ever since—as though what was "right" and what was "wrong" were neatly and clearly discernible, like a slice of black cake against a slice of white. But of course the slices were not nearly so plainly distinguishable as all that. What he had done he had had to do, and it would live long after him. But *how* he had done it would, in retrospect and in some instances, honor his purposes more than his performance. He had been a strong President; and it is a sound stereotype that in all our history only strong Presidents have realized the full capabilities of the office in aid of the general interest. What is not often said, but what is equally true, however, is that there are long-run as well as short-run criteria in these matters. The ablest *politicians* prefer the short-run; and there is much to be said for their choice, as there was specifically for Roosevelt's. But wiser *Presidents* will on the whole prefer the long-run; even though in certain sets of circumstances there is much to be said against such a choice.

Chapter

Sixteen

The one uniquely creative gift of the Anglo-American order to the world's politics is that mysterious thing inside most great Anglo-American statesmen which informs them intuitively of when and where they ought to relax their pressure on their opposition, even when that opposition is manifestly powerless to halt any or all of their current designs. It is this innate quality, a thing of the marrow and spirit, which in all its long centuries has permitted Anglo-American politics to avoid, with rare exceptions like the American Civil War, a politics of a savage and wasting violence expressed in bloody revolutions or in mob actions. It is this thing or quality on which rests at last the whole spirit of government by consent. It is this thing or quality which forbids a tyranny by majorities against minorities—even against a minority of one solitary man. It is this which animates the best and only truly indispensable part of the American Constitution—the Bill of Rights, in which individual, solitary man is made secure in certain rights even if everybody else in the country should disagree with this individual man and wish to do him in.

And it is this innate capacity to turn the cutoff valve, before opposition is not merely defeated but also ground up and destroyed, which is the very mind and heart of all parliamentary systems. (Opposition must not be finally destroyed; for opposition is an irreplaceable part of majority government itself, as it is the only spokesman of the minority claimant to

government.) All this Roosevelt's great wartime comrade
Churchill had always known; not in the sense that he had read
about it or even deeply thought about it. It was simply *in*
him, much as was his command of his native language. All
this Roosevelt's undistinguished successor, Truman, well
knew too, if only because he had learned his lesson as a member of the Senate—the place to which his nostalgia returned
on this day of the funeral procession, as always it was to do
in his years to come, in the White House.

But not all of this had Roosevelt known. As the subtlest
politician of his century he had known when to turn the
cutoff valve so as not to break up public opposition altogether.
He had not, however, grasped the necessary corollary—that
the Congress is the sole home, in the American system, of
this Anglo-American creation of government by consent.

And in his dealings with Congress he had never known at
all how and when to turn the cutoff valve. In his understandable impatience with the hesitations in the old Court
which had amounted, sometimes at least, to actual obstruc-
tionism, he had remade the old Court into the new Court.
And in his contempt for the undoubted weaknesses and ob-
liquely diffused power of the Congress (which also had undoubtedly great reserves of useful strength irreplaceable in
the American system) he had wounded the institution of
Congress itself.

All this he had done for manifestly good purposes. But
there was no point in denying (even as death was casting
upon him the specially ennobling light which death always
casts upon great men at the point of their departure from
life) that in giving a country much he had taken much away.

In the century and a half that had passed before he reached
the Presidency the Congress had always been accepted as
preeminently the people's forum and the ultimate expression
of the people's will. In all the decades before him—in the eras

of strong Presidents as well as in the eras of weaker Presidents
—this tradition, at least, had remained constant.

Roosevelt, on the contrary, had consistently treated Congress not as a respected antagonist in an endless and lawful and inevitable struggle between the separate and coequal powers, but often as actually a kind of openly identified enemy not really worthy of the dignity of office. Toward the old ultimate symbol of popular government, the Congress, he had fostered a vast, and on the whole an uninformed, popular disrespect which was to have many harmful consequences. The dead President had a hundred times put into the minds of his followers the implicit notion not simply that Congress was always slow and "inefficient," as sometimes in fact it was, but also that Congress had no real concern for the people's needs and rights. A man who is one of the three joint trustees of an art gallery will not wisely encourage the people to show their enthusiasm for the paintings he likes by inciting the people to cut up and deface such paintings in the gallery as he himself does not happen to like.

To put the thing another way, when a government is in three inseverable parts, the head of each part owes to the others certain unavoidable obligations. He owes it to them not to set popular passions going against them by fomenting angry oversimplifications which are not only unfair in themselves but hurtful in the end to the whole merged complex of the government itself and thus to the ultimate interests of the people themselves.

Roosevelt, in plain truth, had beset the men of Congress with many aggressions upon their rightful powers and upon their rightful place and dignity. Aggression invites counter-aggression. This is the more so when aggression is essentially unjustified. And it was even the more so in this case, where a President had so repeatedly challenged not merely those opposition members of Congress who were neither of his party nor of his convictions but often substantially the whole of Congress taken as an institution. The blows he had so frequently and so gustily struck had fallen, as the expression goes in reference to the rain, upon the just and unjust alike; upon Democrat as upon Republican; upon liberal, conservative, and reactionary Congressmen alike.

The analogy of the brilliant but not overly thoughtful captain, the assault commander, which rose to mind on that day of the funeral procession recurs again and again when one peers back from the afterlight. As has been seen, Roosevelt's war policy had looked too much to the immediate goal, the destruction of military fascism in the world, and too little toward the distant goal, the shape of the world after fascism. Just so, his domestic policies, and most particularly his relationship with the Congress, had looked too much toward the achievement of immediate bread-and-butter objectives and too little toward the distant consequences. He had put the contest with Congress into an unduly harsh, simplistic context in which the here-and-now bulked all too large and the further future of the Republic all too small. (It is, again and again, a pity that his perceptive interest in history had been so small.)

The years of his greatest power—his first two terms—had left a kind of no man's land between his seat at 1600 Pennsylvania Avenue and the seat of Congress in the large, bulbous structure, known as the Capitol, at the other end of that Avenue. Most of Congress felt that it had been overrun and occupied—and most of Congress was not altogether wrong. So it was that even before the accident of death the forces of Congress had been slowly and implacably marshaling for a sustained—and what was sometimes to be a terrible—counteroffensive to recover the lost ground which the Executive had wrested from the Legislature. He had departed from the Constitution in carrying forward his campaign, often impatiently substituting the cold imperatives of "must" for the warmer and no less effective (if slower) processes of persuasion that end in consent. Now, *they* would depart from the Constitution. He had expanded the Presidential power too far; they were now going to cut it back too much. He had acted with purposes that never were evil and always were in pursuit of what he had thought to be the people's higher interests. But he had caused deep injury to Congress, and over this injury Congressional memory would linger long; and it would be resolved in Congress that it must never happen again. Not many years later, for a single illustration, Congress would overwhelmingly submit and the states would overwhelmingly ratify a Constitutional amendment forever forbidding to any President any service beyond two terms.

But in the meantime look backward in time again to the gray, compact man riding, as though all alone, in the funeral coach behind the body of Franklin D. Roosevelt as now the caisson approached the White House where the ancient service for the dead was to roll out in all its clipped, somber power for an Episcopalian (no longer a President) whose race had been run.

Harry Truman had been himself a man of Congress. And it was widely reckoned among the politically sophisticated, even on that day when all but a small part of men's minds was turned to mourning and not to speculation, that the new President Truman would restore an Executive-Legislative relationship which the old President had so deeply harmed. Even the people generally—not excluding those many millions who yesterday had gaily shared FDR's very dim view of Congressional rights—would now begin to feel a nostalgia for a lost system which, however misty and obscure in their minds, they would now begin to miss. To be sure, they did not fully comprehend just what it was that had been damaged, and how, in their national life. Those dusty, fusty "checks and balances" were not now, of course, suddenly and in clear understanding, being reembraced like members of the family coming home from the wars. No, it did not go nearly so far as this; it would be much too fanciful to say that it did.

There was, however, a wide, very imperfect, instinctive sensing that there had been some deep disharmony, some disunion, in the great house of government. And there was, to this small and carefully qualified extent, some vague, instinctive hope that now all this would be put aright by a new President whose homely virtues were thought of then as also quite limited virtues largely confined to moderation in view and a certain pedestrian and undemanding political knowhow. Well, this man has *been* in Congress; *he* will know how to get along with Congress, at all events.

But it had been Roosevelt who had sown the wind; it was now to be Truman (and through him the United States of America) who would reap the whirlwind.

In warfare victories over enemy forces are often inadmissible and undesirable if they are to be had only at the cost of intolerable casualties among one's own troops. In politics, in statecraft, there is a profound, controlling principle quite to the reverse: Certain victories must not be won at undue cost in casualties among the opposition. For the ultimate aim of politics is to bind together for common purposes those contending forces which for a time, in the intermediate phases of the action, must be set one against the other. For, unlike warfare, there are in Western politics properly no *enemies* within the state; there are only *opponents*. And the whole final purpose of the game is to overcome the opponents, or a good clutch of them at any rate, as a mere necessary preliminary to making yesterday's antagonist the recruit of tomorrow. Statecraft, that is to say, properly involves a highly civilized contest; war is the ultimate in incivility.

Chapter

Seventeen

So it was that the new President, Truman, would have at once to face a bleak and irreparable reality. The institution of Congress had now dug in against the institution of the Presidency in the spirit not of an opponent, but rather in the spirit of an enemy. No longer would it be possible to accommodate the great issue lying between the one and the other; now it was to be war. The erstwhile man of Congress now residing in the White House was about to face a long storm of a violent, often an automatic, and for years an unthinkably extreme antagonism from Capitol Hill.

As has already been seen, the erstwhile majority party—which was nominally a Democratic Party but actually far more a *Roosevelt*-Democratic Party—could be neither a unified nor an effective force from the moment Roosevelt died. Stripped thus of the supporting partisan army upon which one Democratic President succeeding another Democratic President might normally have counted, Truman had now few arms to take up in a swiftly rising sea of troubles. The bellicose Congress would, almost as though by an act of instinct, find its allies wherever it could. No matter how uncomfortably the ideas and ideals generally of some of these allies would clash with the ideas and ideals generally of what was to be, for a short time, still nominally a Democratic Congress, the basic point was this: The hunt was up for the institution of the Presidency. The mere Roosevelt-haters among politicians and public, whose motive was never the large one of restoring a right Executive-Legislative relationship but only the small one of besmirching Roosevelt's memory—even these would do for the moment as allies.

So it was that Truman, as now the occupant of the Presidency, was to become the hunted in a long and terrible time of trial for the American Presidency. No one could possibly measure in those times (and no one even now can possibly measure) the full consequences of this tragic era. Where an old President had been allowed to do all that he chose—or had forced upon Congress an acceptance of all that he chose—a new President was to be allowed to do almost nothing at all except in that area of affairs, foreign policy, where no Congress could have checked his acts in any case. Roosevelt had oversimplified both the facts and the nature of the Constitutional structure of government in order to do what he had thought it necessary to do.

Now Congress was to oversimplify in the same way. Roosevelt had demanded too much; Truman was to be denied too much. When there is unduly hard action there is harder reaction. When there is extremism in a good cause there will be extremism in an exceedingly bad cause—or, rather, in an essentially good cause fatally marred by malignant men who have joined this cause for malignant and petty reasons of their own.

For Truman was to find that, in his hands and not through any fault of his, the Presidency simply would not work— except beyond the seas, where with matchless sturdiness and wistful gallantry he was to assume the vital headship of a Western world whose chief nation, the United States, he would never be allowed really to lead.

A Congress that would tear each and every one of his major

domestic programs apart, right or wrong, good or bad, would not be able to prevent his salvation of Greece and Turkey; his introduction of the Marshall Plan; his carving of that immense monument to rational planning and rational strength, the North Atlantic Treaty Organization; his plunge into Korea to save something (but unhappily never all) of the free world's position in the Orient.

The great struggle between the Congress and the Presidency was to bring unconstitutional Congressional attacks on undoubtedly Constitutional Presidential powers, particularly in the Senate. A President's demonstrable right to send divisions of troops to Europe under NATO, as an obviously proper function of a President acting as Commander in Chief, was, for example, to be endlessly and damagingly debated as though the President of the United States was some shabby trickster claiming an office that might not really exist. The troops would at length be sent; but their mission would not go unharmed.

First from Congress itself and then all across the land there was to spread a miasma of hate and fear and suspicion not ever before to fall so widely or so cruelly upon the country. All this mixed band of attackers—the Congress, which on the whole was seeking, if the wrong way, to reclaim its rightful powers; the Roosevelt-haters in their simple malice, and the far-right-wingers in general—was to raise serious question as to the ability of the United States government really to govern.

It would become possible for a bitter isolationist Senator to call General of the Army George C. Marshall a "front man for traitors"—that Marshall who had so helped win the war, that Marshall whose whole life had been one of a lofty patriotism! It would become not merely possible but commonplace for the honor of the country itself in the war years—in the negotiations with Japan before Pearl Harbor; in the unwise but surely honorable dealings of Roosevelt at the Yalta Conference and elsewhere—to be brought under openly slanderous attack.

There would be a long and evil search for evil motives where only mistakes had existed; there would be an unendingly savage cross fire between Capitol and White House in which partisans among the public community would take up their places in ambush like guerrillas behind the scrabbly hedgerows. The Democratic Party would now fall wholly apart in wasting, puerile quarreling within itself—so much so that a sitting President of the United States, Mr. Truman, would be nominated for a full term by the Democrats in 1948 only because a man named Eisenhower (not then either quite a Democrat or quite a Republican) could not readily be had for the job. This sitting President of the United States would be kept waiting for hours past midnight on the sooty ironstairway fretwork of a Democratic National Convention in Philadelphia to accept his nomination, like a messenger boy calling for a telegram which was being written without regard to his comfort or his time.

The Republican Party, for its part, was to become for years the forum not of policies but only of bitter philippics; a posse of pseudo sheriffs trailing a sort of Presidential bandit and a political party of outlaws across the blighted landscape.

It was to be an era of a savage presumptuousness toward the Presidential office which this country had not known since the worst part of Lincoln's time.

In all this, what was Truman to do—what could he do? He was to open in the 1948 Presidential campaign a somewhat mechanical attack upon the institution that was so determined in one way or another to destroy him. He was to call this, the Eightieth Congress, "the worst" ever. And some were to delude themselves into thinking that it was this charge and this technique that had returned him to the White House. It would not be this, of course; it would not be anything that Truman had done or not done, said or not said. It would not be that he had won; it would be only that the Republican Presidential nominee, Thomas E. Dewey of New York, had with unexampled maladroitness defeated himself.

And Truman, at the end of his service, would be repudiated in the 1952 Presidential campaign upon grounds so totally and mutually contradictory as to add a unique chapter to the history of political irony: He had been "too soft" on Communism, and he had persisted too much in killing aggressive Communists in Korea—all at once.

But turn the mind back again for a moment to the procession now drawing up at the gates of the White House, there to deliver the body of Franklin Roosevelt on that day so long ago. It was here that many things were ending, in loss and in sorrow; but it was here, too, that some things were beginning. Among these beginnings, though surely no one could sense it on that day, was a slowly unfolding, still unformed, feeling among the public that, grieve for him as they did, they had done for a while with strong Presidents and now would require one not exactly weak but a little bit so.

They were to try—public and Congress—to make the immediately new President, Truman, into this ambiguous mold. They were not to succeed in this—they would beat him about the head, but his head would remain stubbornly upright, so that men could later say of him, as I have said here of him, that he was a great President in the transcendent things but a poor President in the small things; and in all things an indifferent politician, at the most generous estimate. But they—public and Congress—were to have their way, a little later. For to this design, to which they were already turning without knowing it and which they were later to execute still without really knowing it, the President now dead had surely led them, though this was surely the last thing he ever would consciously have done.

I recoil, as it happens, from discussing what are called "spiritual values" in politics. Even the word "moral" as used explicitly in this connection I find a little embarrassing and sticky. But I do believe that at rare times a spirit in some strange and almost mystical way will move among the public, informing them as it moves—informing them not necessarily in the right way, but informing them nevertheless. And abroad this day, I think, was a spirit which, born in fatigue, now sought only rest; which, born in strife, now sought only peace; which, born in heroism, now sought only the lap of compromise and inaction.

The very man being mourned this day had uniquely expressed those strenuous qualities of strength and risk which were now to be put aside; these qualities we were preparing to bury even as we were preparing to bury him. In an especially deep sense it was, indeed, "Hail Roosevelt—Roosevelt farewell." Nearly every facet of his shining, demanding personality had bitten deep into the national consciousness—and into the national unconscious. Now that his life was at an end, sorrow was running a curious race this day with quite another emotion. This was the emotion of unexpressed relief that not soon would the country be again so compelled—to effort, to struggle, to controversy and contention—as this man had so long compelled it.

Not often, I think, had all our old expressions for death— the broken vessel; the turning from flesh to clay; the terrible, lonely refrain "ashes to ashes, dust to dust"—been so profoundly, so bleakly, so chokingly apt as on this day. This body of a man who only yesterday had been so powerful a

President, who in his mind and person had been the locus of
the energy and force of half a world, what did it now repre-
sent? In an instant, there was no longer the power, no longer
the glory. Never, surely, had we seen how immense, how
infinite, lies the gulf between what, in the old rubrics, were
called the quick and the dead. They were taking this body
into the White House now. But they were not taking there
what remained of a great public man; they were taking there,
for the oddly humble petitions of his church, what remained
of a private man who was being by others commended to
the mercies of a God to Whom he himself could never try to
speak again on this side of whatever immortal place or time
or space may lie beyond.

As a public man he had fought the good fight; he had run
the good race. But in this funeral service there was no longer
anything to do, really, with the public, nothing to do with
powers and principalities, in what was being said. Now, in
the last privacy, the privacy of death, there fell away all the
princely trappings—and from those within the White House
mourning groups fell away all thought of such trappings—of
public office and public renown. The only office left here
was an office not to be held but to be performed, the Office
of the Dead simply for a member of the Episcopal Church
who had been called Franklin Delano Roosevelt; who had
been born, who had lived a while, and who had died, in the
slow, inevitable succession of those seasons which are the
beginning, the middle and then the end.

Chapter

Eighteen

Here on that April day, in the East Room of the White House, a room that had known all grandeur and sadness, all hope and conclusion, the walls were covered with the soft flowers of the spring of a coming peace in this land and all about the world. And, with a fittingness which caught at the senses, the world's secular Easter was arriving upon the heels of a departure—not, certainly, of a god, but of a man stoutly full in his life of man's secular and mortal imperfections, but a man all the same who had done the best he could, on the whole, for those who had shared his country with him.

The coffin lay wrapped in the flag of the United States. President Truman sat there in somber silence. So did Anthony Eden of Britain, who himself was later to reach his own country's highest office and then to lose it tragically in a dissonance within the Western Alliance—this one over British interest in the Suez—which would have its real roots in the easy anticolonialism of the man now dead in this room. So sat Mrs. Roosevelt and other members of the family whose rather casually generous and absent-mindedly patriarchal head had now gone.

It was an hour for both a formal expression of stately grief for reasons of state and a genuine expression of personal grief. At that hour not Eden himself and not any other man could have known that within a few years this chief deputy of old Churchill would find his career destroyed and the long Anglo-

American comradeship brutally and dangerously embittered by the fruits of Franklin Roosevelt's anticolonialism. Who could have supposed that in 1956 the United States of America would join the Soviet Union in condemning in the United Nations the effort of these British friends—and of our French and Israeli friends as well—to dash the hands of Colonel Nasser of Egypt from their throats as those hands of good "nationalism" and "independence" were closing on the Suez Canal? True, it was to be in Eisenhower's administration that we would support the Russians in denouncing as aggressive invasion this convulsive leap of our friends into Egypt to meet the peril demonstrably gathering about their vitals in the Middle East.

But the unalterable philosophy lying behind this extraordinary American action—which among other things would in the end drive Eden a sick and broken man from the prime-ministership—had been made and imbedded in national opinion long before Eisenhower would doff his battle jacket. It had been so made and so imbedded by Franklin Roosevelt. Even during the war then ending he had over and over insisted upon policies and actions which would strip the exhausted and blooded British of those very foreign positions and quasi possessions through which alone could they even hope to draw economic revivification to a shattered homeland and home economy.

It is of course true that the long movement of history— and no doubt all the considerations of abstract justice—would in any event have meant the end, in time, of colonialism. But Roosevelt had persisted in demanding much too much, much too soon, driven as he was by a suspicion of the clever, the tricky British that was almost a schoolboy's stereotype; by an almost incredibly naïve belief that since they voted in Massachusetts they must vote *at once* in Sudan; by a kind of highly simplified "good guy" political view which he would have scorned as wholly puerile in any domestic context.

So it was that in the East Room of the White House on that elegiac afternoon the shadows of the future were almost as much at hand—though not of course readily discernible—as were the sorrows of the present and the pervasive memories of the recent past of a man now dead. But in that room, too, were the ancestral, the spiritual, the long memories of the long past. And now these were brought forth in a Spartan parade in the liturgy of Roosevelt's church.

The Right Reverend Angus Dun of the Episcopal Diocese of Washington stood, in a bleak absence of all pomp and of any undue posturing before death, to give the Church's farewell to the man who had made his own gay Pilgrim's Progress, with all its strength and all its faltering and weakness, in the timeless tradition of that timeless thing, the English-speaking world, whose strength has forever been its arrogance but whose glory has forever been its unshakable conviction of the value of every single man.

There were two hymns which had been the dead President's favorites—"Eternal Father Strong to Save" and "Faith of Our Fathers." All in the East Room—about two hundred men and women were gathered there—sang, their quiet, mannered voices rising to the three great crystal chandeliers which lit a scene of equally mannered melancholy.

The thought crossed my mind—and it lingers to this day—that it is not, at the end, a man's public importance which matters. For when death comes, there comes the necessity of a reckoning, a balancing, an estimating of a man's public life which will have only such meaning as each reckoner, each balancer, each estimator, may choose to give it, in his own way and in his own time. What matters at the end, as it seemed to me on that day, and now, is the degree of gallantry, of principle, of compassion and of truth which, President or infantry rifleman, king or unemployed miner, the dead man had put into the adventure now drawn in unutterable enigma and in unbroken mystery to its close.

This, at any rate, is what Roosevelt's church thought of this occasion. For it spoke not of a man who had been a President but only of a man—a man whose need of the common prayers of the survivors was manifest and traditional.

I am the Resurrection and the life, saith the Lord: He that believeth in Me, though he were dead, yet he shall live: And whosoever liveth and believeth in Me shall never die.

I know that my Redeemer liveth, and that He shall stand at the latter day upon the earth; and though this body be destroyed, yet shall I see God: Whom I shall see for myself, and mine eyes shall behold, and not as a stranger.

We brought nothing into this world, and it is certain we can carry nothing out. The Lord gave, and the Lord hath taken away; blessed be the name of the Lord.

So intoned Bishop Dun as the shadows now entered the room and as the past now came wholly to drive away the present and, for these moments, even the future too.

And when the Bishop had done, his lesser clerical companions thus went on:

God is our hope and strength, a very present help in trouble.

Therefore we will not fear, though the earth be moved, and though the hills be carried into the midst of the sea;

Though the waters thereof rage and swell, and though the mountains shake at the tempest of the same.

There is a river, the streams whereof make glad the city of God; the holy place of the tabernacle of the Most Highest . . .

Be still then, and know that I am God: I will be exalted among the nations, and I will be exalted in the earth.

The Lord of hosts is with us; the God of Jacob is our refuge . . .

I will lift up mine eyes unto the hills; from whence cometh my help.

My help cometh even from the Lord, Who hath made heaven and earth.

He will not suffer thy foot to be moved; and He that keepeth thee will not sleep.

Behold, He that keepeth Israel shall neither slumber nor sleep.

The Lord Himself is thy keeper, the Lord is thy defence upon thy right hand;

So that the sun shall not burn thee by day, neither the moon by night.

The Lord shall preserve thee from all evil; yea, it is even He that shall keep thy soul.

The Lord shall preserve thy going out, and thy coming in, from this time forth for evermore . . .

As many as are led by the Spirit of God, they are the sons of God. For ye have not received the spirit of adoption, whereby we cry, Abba, Father. The Spirit Himself beareth witness with our spirit, that we are the children of God; and if children, then heirs; heirs of God, and joint-heirs with Christ; if so be that we suffer with Him, that we may be also glorified together. For I reckon that the sufferings of this present time are not worthy to be compared with the glory which shall be revealed in us. For the earnest expectation of the creature waiteth for the manifestation of the Son of God. We know that all things work together for good to them that love God, to them who are the called according to His purpose. What shall we then say to these things? If God be for us, who can be against us? He that spared not His own Son, but delivered Him up for us all, how shall He not with Him also freely give us all things? Who is he that condemneth? It is Christ that died, yea rather, that is risen

again, Who is even at the right hand of God, Who also maketh
intercession for us. Who shall separate us from the love of
Christ? Shall tribulation, or distress, or persecution, or famine,
or nakedness, or peril, or sword? Nay, in all these things we
are more than conquerors through Him that loved us. For
I am persuaded that neither death, nor life, nor angels, nor
principalities, nor powers, nor things present, nor things to
come, nor height, nor depth, nor any other creature, shall
be able to separate us from the love of God, which is in
Christ Jesus our Lord . . .

Jesus said, Let not your heart be troubled; ye believe in
God, believe also in Me. In my Father's house are many man-
sions; if it were not so, I would have told you. I go to pre-
pare a place for you. And if I go and prepare a place for
you, I will come again, and receive you unto Myself; that
where I am, there ye may be also. And whither I go ye know,
and the way ye know. Thomas saith unto Him, Lord, we
know not whither Thou goest; and how can we know the
way? Jesus saith unto him, I am the way, the truth, and the
life: no man cometh unto the Father, but by Me.

Thus ran the ancient words of comfort—and they were of
comfort to those who did not quite believe them traditionally
almost as much as to those who did believe them in just that
way. This, however, was far from the kind of comfort which
in the broad and public sense would now descend upon the
country Roosevelt had left. True, his ending had been, here
in the brief moments of the funeral in the White House, the
ending not of a great public official but only of a private man.
But the unalterable fact remained that to the nation at large
it was still a farewell not to a private man but to a public man
and to a span and kind of national public life that would come
no more.

Chapter

Nineteen

The kind of pervasive comfort now to come upon us—or, rather, to be demanded by us—would be characterized by a political softness at home accompanying the kind of foreign-policy sentimentalism abroad that would be consistently expressed in the destruction, one by one, of the offshore positions of strength that had been held by our allies, like Eden's Britain.

For we were going to be hell-bent on the easy way, in our national political life no less than in our personal lives. Truman's foredoomed efforts at maintaining a real and thrusting domestic leadership would break upon more than the rock of an institutional Congressional hostility really directed primarily not at Truman but at the memory of Roosevelt's policy of demanding rather than persuading.

These efforts would break also upon a spongy, but nevertheless unyielding, mass of public yearning for a total ease and an increasing public distaste for all forensics and contentiousness in politics. A whole generation of lesser but still important public leaders was passing along with Roosevelt himself. In its place a new generation of young or younger leaders was arising. But, with surpassing oddity, it would turn out that these new young, or comparatively young, men of power would show more of the characteristics of age—caution, care, nonbelligerency in life—than had the old men now departing the national scene.

For some of the wide variety of legacies—both desirable and undesirable—that had been left by the death in Warm Springs I have assigned here a measure of praise or blame directly to Roosevelt himself. In this instance—in the instance of this ambiguous legacy of a new politics of comfort but not of creativity—I do not know how to assign quite what to the dead President. For one thing, there is an immense and, to me, an unanswerable question as to whether the new politics should be considered on the whole good or bad; perhaps one should say that it was both good and bad. At any rate, one must say that it was inevitable. (And *is* inevitable and enduring, for it was this kind of politics, basically, which dominated a Presidential election so recently as the year 1960.)

The law of physics by which action will create reaction was never morely clearly illustrated, in political terms, than here. In the words of the funeral services there had surely been tribulation, and distress, and famine, and nakedness, and peril and sword in the years of Roosevelt in the White House. And, surely, too, there had also been those sufferings of a "present time" of which the Office of the Dead had made its traditional mention.

At all these evils and dangers the dead President had struck with a gallant gusto—but at them, too, he had sometimes struck with more vigor than wisdom. For thirteen years he had kept his nation drawn up in a universal, unslackening tenseness against unending crises, at home, abroad. The national mind, the very national muscle, had long been drawn into knotted cords. The Depression had been met and at length mastered. The war had been confronted and was now being won. The social landscape had been deeply altered—and no such alteration could be made without human cost.

The whole country was now in that state of a feverish fatigue which will result from the very sudden ending of long and high and demanding endeavor. If it was not tired of Roosevelt the Just, it was tired of Roosevelt the Doer; it wanted now no doers; it wanted relaxers in the high positions of state. It wanted an end of parades; it wanted to lie on the grass in the back yard. It wanted no stentorian political voices calling for sacrifice and exertion; it wanted mild, bland voices speaking of accommodation, of leisure, of the good life in a world now made safe from more or less everything.

So it was that the whole political reason and operating method of Roosevelt's being was passing even as he himself was passing into the past. The luckless Truman—and no man in history had ever ascended to the Presidency with the circumstances of fate more massively arrayed against him and his tenure—now confronted what Grover Cleveland had liked to call a condition and not a theory. The theory was that the people had desired a strong President; the fact was that in Roosevelt's time they simply had had to have such a one. But the new condition was that they did not desire and would not accept a strong President—and Truman never was to know how to be a weak one.

It may seem an arbitrary view, but in the long slope of history one must consider the Truman years now opening to have been, domestically, only a forced liquidation of an old public phase by a successor who really wanted not to end it at all but rather to deepen and expand it. At home, he would be able to demand nothing of a people which had had its fill of all demands. He would sit for years in a White House as an occupant more tolerated by his people than accepted as their leader. He would find all avenues of real domestic headship closed to him. He would then, with much courage and even greater skill, turn to the headship of the many nations which desperately required a headship to save them from the red fascists who had done so much to help in the execution of the brown fascist Hitler.

He would become, that is to say, the President of the Free World—but never quite the President of the United States. And as he would see the steady disintegration of the always illogical but once immensely powerful Roosevelt-Democratic Party, with nothing organizationally at hand to replace it, he would see the emergence of the new politics of compromise, the new politics of an ever expanding center and of ever contracting left and right wings.

For, by rich irony, the most powerful Democratic President who had ever held office, Roosevelt, had opened the way to the most significant and the most enduring weakening processes in the old-style party system that we had ever known. He had conducted himself, as party leader and as national leader, so as to depreciate the concept of the supremacy of the *Democratic* Party in favor of the *Roosevelt*-Democratic Party. This was essentially a short-term coalition dedicated to the current, and mainly emergency, legislative and policy achievements of Franklin D. Roosevelt. This coalition had no genuine purpose to forward the Democratic Party as a party. Indeed, FDR had never been a partisan in accepted terms; and the country in his time itself had ceased being partisan in those terms. One became pro-Roosevelt or anti-Roosevelt; few remained, at the time of his death, who were simply pro-Democratic or pro-Republican. In his kind of purely personal leadership he had repeatedly made pragmatic alliances with liberal Republicans in the Senate and House and elsewhere, at the direct expense of traditional Democrats. (For one characteristic example, he had the late Senator George W. Norris of Nebraska, a maverick Republican who was liberal in domestic views and reactionary-

isolationist in world affairs, introduce the bill that created
the Tennessee Valley Authority. He thus bypassed, and forever and damagingly offended, old Senator Kenneth McKellar of Tennessee, who was to spend many subsequent years
exacting a recurring revenge from his powerful seat as chairman of the Senate Appropriations Committee. The same bill
could have been as well had from McKellar and much trouble
for the future thus avoided.)

A man always in a hurry, FDR wanted always, and only,
results. So it was that because there was much that was evil
(and also much that was simply annoying and embarrassing
to him) in the old big-city machines, he had set out one by
one to destroy them. He had unhesitatingly smashed Democratic centers of local or regional political power whenever
and wherever, on one or another of his current designs, they
were not *Roosevelt*-Democratic centers of power. In the end,
for example, he had broken up nearly every effective Democratic organization in his own home state of New York, thus
opening the opportunity for an immense resurgence of the
Republicans which in turn led to the Dewey-Rockefeller era,
an era that has, even now in 1961, by no means run its course.

In all this, as in some other things, including his essential
views of foreign policy, can be seen the strong strain of oversimplification that had run in this man for whom the old
prayers were now being said. (And in all this—and not solely
in their disagreement with his policies—lay a good part of
the explanation for the progressive expendability of FDR's
original party associates as his first term had lengthened into
a second, a third and a fourth. Old Jim Farley had not parted
with Roosevelt exclusively because he demanded a third term;
there was also here an increasing disenchantment by a good
party man, Farley, with a President who had thought less and
less of that party and more and more of the *Roosevelt* party.

So, too, with some of the Southern right-wingers, James F. Byrnes of South Carolina among them.)

For FDR's real opinion of his party, and of the whole party structure as we had long known it, had been revealed again and again in his essential lack of sympathy with parliamentary government even in the very qualified sense that such a form of government could be said to be involved in our system. His was, really, the government of a man who superimposed himself upon a system. It was by no means "undemocratic"; indeed, it was highly democratic, for his whole operating method rested infinitely more upon the consent of the people than upon the consent of the people's representatives—in Congress and in the courts. No President had ever been so profoundly democratic, in the root meaning of that word; no President had ever been so profoundly unrepublican, in the root meaning of that word. Thus it was that no President had ever been more unconsciously destructive of his own party. For the parties, though nowhere mentioned in the Constitution, had for nearly a century been in truth the basic means by which representative government was carried on. He had expended his party as he often had expended his Cabinet friendships. He had never done this except in pursuit of what he actually believed was (and probably really was) the overriding public interest. But done it he had, and now the consequences would begin to emerge.

He had habituated the people to voting not for parties but for men—in his case, for one man—and it would turn out that the lesson had gone deeply home. Once Truman had served his tour of duty, revolutionary forms of voting would begin to appear among a public now incomparably more concerned about personalities than about parties. It would then follow as a corollary that an electorate judging upon the basis almost wholly of men would require those who sought the

Presidency to seek favor as men and not as partisan, that is to say party, leaders.

And in turn it would follow that the ostensible comparative strength of the parties, as measured by what beforehand had been such very nearly controlling criteria as total party registration, would have less and less meaning. Presidential aspirants would necessarily begin to offer themselves as pretty much all things to all men. And as they would begin so to offer themselves, it would be inevitable that they would propose more the policies of consensus and accommodation than the sharply competing two sets of policies which we had usually known in the past.

Chapter

Twenty

It would become possible for us to look backward in 1960—
when Richard Nixon for the Republicans and John F. Kennedy for the Democrats were running on official convention
platforms that were quite different but on real and actual
personal platforms that were different more in detail than in
principle—and to say this: Not since 1940, when Wendell
Willkie had in vain challenged FDR, had the country seen
a truly clear-cut Presidential contest in terms of party col-
lision.

And, as early as 1952, Roosevelt's appointed field captain
in the war, Dwight Eisenhower, would give the most perfect
illustration possible of the new politics of quiet and accommodation. He would win the Presidency in a victory for a pro-
Eisenhower coalition but in a nonvictory for the Republican
Party and a nondefeat for the Democratic Party. He would
go on then, though in the meantime he had been so gravely
ill as to raise perfectly sound and objective fears that he well
might not survive it, to win a second term in a great landslide
—a landslide, that is, for Dwight Eisenhower. For this time
his party would do so poorly as to set up a historic negative
benchmark in politics. The man who had won so tremendous
and so theoretical a Republican victory would see the voters
return both houses of Congress to Democratic control.

And this would also follow, in the days and years from

this funeral in the White House to the present time: The new young men of the Democratic Party, accompanied by its few surviving elders in places of power, would reject the combativeness of Roosevelt's operating techniques even as they emulated his form of personal appeal in recruiting public support to reach office. For once the Truman interregnum had ended and the long Eisenhower era had opened, these young and highly responsible Democrats—who were to be Eisenhower's official opposition—would look beyond Eisenhower to the country. Where Roosevelt had smiled and lashed his critics, they would smile and enfold and encircle their critics. Where he had divided the country they would draw it together. They would not fight Eisenhower. Instead they would assist Eisenhower, not because they feared his competence but because they thought him rather incompetent and felt their obligation to a people and not very much to a party which FDR himself had taught them to regard as a factor of ever shifting and ambiguous value in a national political equation.

Not wholly accidentally, these new young men of the Democratic Party would be both liberal and conservative, not in cynicism but in actual fact. They would find their essential leadership among Southerners or the Western types (with some rare exceptions) like Senators Lyndon B. Johnson of Texas and Mike Mansfield of Montana. For it had been the South assisted by the ill-populated West, which had produced the doctrine of the concurrent majority (by way of a creative South Carolina politician named John Calhoun, who is thereby on the Senate's official roster of the five greatest Senators of all time in spite of the stain of his proslavery views). The sense of this doctrine was that on issues of great public passion accommodations should be made by which a momentary majority would restrain itself from pressing upon momentary minorities acts and policies which were truly intolerable (not merely repugnant) to those minorities.

Now the new Southern and Western Democrats, Johnson at the forefront among them, would prepare a new concept of majority which would, by 1960, actually invest the thinking of both parties, and in nearly all their geographic sections. This concept of majority would be subtle and fluid and in the deepest way it would influence both Republican Presidential candidate Nixon and Democratic Presidential candidate Kennedy in 1960. Its very framers, again notably Johnson, would not attempt explicitly or consciously to define it. But, in my own definition, it would come to this: The ideal, the end purpose, of the new majority was not so much to protect the minority, as was Calhoun's; it was to set up such a condition of affairs in national politics that the majority, if quite loosely formed, would so burgeon as to form, for practical purposes, nearly the whole body of the electorate. In a word, ideally there would be left scarcely any resisting minority worthy of the name. The old social legislation contests of Roosevelt's time, for illustration, would never again generate one tenth their original heat; many issues would be assumed, by both parties, to have been so settled in principle that only detail would be left to be argued.

The Democratic Party, post-Roosevelt, would not in fact be able again to call itself "the party of the poor." Nor would it be able again to denounce the Republican Party as the "party of the rich." Now it would be a case in which the Democratic Party was a party of some of the poor, many of the middle class, and some of the rich—and a case in which the Republican Party was almost precisely the same thing. And (an important point it is, too) there would be this: "The poor"—in our old definition of that term—would become an obsolescent slogan, anyhow.

The consequences of this extraordinary condition of affairs would, of course, be many. And they would be of mixed value; partly good for the country, partly bad for it. The hatreds Roosevelt had engendered among a very powerful minority wholly united upon this point if on no other would be quite as lasting as would be the love he had evoked from an otherwise disparate majority. Thus the strong tendency of the new politics to dispel and to diffuse passion and heat in public affairs (I speak here of the period which would open out after the Truman interregnum) would be enormously beneficial to the country; it would lie like a cooling poultice over the brow of fever. Indeed, the first technically non-Democratic but actually coalition Administration to follow the Roosevelt Revolution, the initial term of General Eisenhower as President, would be notable principally—and almost exclusively—for this: Nothing would be done by its head or by it which could be even remotely described as involving a powerful or demanding or creative act of leadership. But everything that would be done—or, as was often the case, not done—would carry forward the new concept of the politics of compromise and calm.

Would McCarthyism—the twentieth-century know-nothingism of a swarthy Senator from Wisconsin named Joseph McCarthy—become a bitter problem in the late Forties and early Fifties? Indeed it would. But how would this problem be approached by the Eisenhower Administration? Where Roosevelt would have grappled with it instantly and with a total, hostile commitment of mind and emotion, Eisenhower would not meet it directly at all. If Roosevelt had considered the Constitution and its careful balance of executive, legislative and judicial power to be more a document than a fact,

Eisenhower would consider it a more compelling and a more unqualified fact than it ever really was.

Roosevelt had read the Constitution very early in his life and had been inclined to regard it much as Herbert Hoover had once regarded Prohibition—an experiment "noble in purpose." But Eisenhower, who had spent decades in the politically undemanding role of a military officer, would turn out to have read the Constitution a good deal too late in his life, and surely a good deal too literally.

Where Roosevelt had so often treated the Congress as a windy and obstructionist nuisance to the things he thought had to be done, Eisenhower would treat Congress rather with the openmouthed awe of a small boy gazing for the first time upon the dubious beauty but undoubted suggestion of power which is the Capitol dome. He would most of the time take the view that Congress was not merely separate from the executive branch, as it was and ought to be, but that the elected head of all the people, the President, had no great responsibility even to attempt to persuade a Congress toward this course or away from that one.

Thus, Eisenhower's role in the crisis of McCarthyism—which was in fact at its height to be a much nastier thing than many sensible people would ever believe—would be precisely in the mood of that uncreative, unurgent public mood which would be expressed in the new politics of accommodation and ease. He would do little about it, one way or the other, except for occasionally and calmly letting it be known that he found it all quite distressing and hoped that in time it would be no more. He would stand, in a word, a full pendulum's stroke away from where Roosevelt had stood; here, as in so much else, one would see how compromise, letting things alone, would succeed action, compelling personal leadership, letting nothing whatever alone.

Nevertheless, the years to come would bring most ample proof that Roosevelt's personalization of the institution of the Presidency had become the towering and central fact of our succeeding politics. If later Presidents would be comparatively weak, or at all events filled with a policy of *laissez faire* as would Eisenhower, for illustration, every succeeding President, all the same, would find himself to be the leader of the nation, whether or not he would have preferred that singular and lonely role. Weak, middling, or strong, he would be required by our new national political mores to be a personal and not an institutional President.

Absently, and with entirely other purposes in mind, FDR had made a whole new political landscape, a whole new political climate in which the parties would enter a long and progressively accelerating decline and in which all traditional forms of collectively partisan action (say as between the Executive and Congressional wings of the same party) would have less and less vitality or meaning.

We should see many proofs of this. Looking back from 1961, for one illustration, it would be clear in retrospect that the last truly powerful and meaningful chairmanship of a national political party had been held by Jim Farley before he broke in 1940 with Roosevelt over the third term and associated issues.

Truman himself would gain election to a full term in 1948 through circumstances, and through his own personal efforts, and Thomas Dewey's incomparable maladroitness, that would have almost no real relationship to a now outmoded instrumentality called the Democratic National Committee. Eisenhower would come forward, in 1952, as a personal candidate for President, appealing to a nonpartisan-minded public, to whom the Republican National Committee was about as relevant—and about as needed—as were relevant to the automobile's performance those little record players which some of our motor manufacturers would install in their sedans in the early Fifties.

Eisenhower himself, as we should see, would have toward the national committee of what was officially his party, the G.O.P., about the degree of attachment that he might have had to the functioning of the stenographic pool in the White House executive office. That is to say, he would have nothing against the Republican National Committee; but he would visibly have some difficulty upon occasion in recalling, off-hand, the name of its current chairman.

So it would turn out that both national committees, all through the Eisenhower years, would become places of an unwitting somnolence. They would go through the old proper motions of promoting partisan operations; the only difficulty would be that partisan operations, in anything like the old definition, would no longer really exist in any true spirit.

Chapter

Twenty-One

The G.O.P. Committee "ins" would, perforce, relax. The Democratic Committee "outs" would not do quite this; they would enter upon a long period of a wistfully feverish threshing-about which, to put the unkindly exact description upon the process, would be full of a sound and fury signifying the most earnest partisan intentions but little else. Once Truman had completed his inherited stint, it would be seen that the new men of the new politics of moderation and accommodation within the Democratic Party would have little time and less use for such hangovers of the past as national committees.

The Democratic Presidential nominee in 1952, Adlai E. Stevenson, would, of course, have a "national committee," but he would make of his *personal* campaign associates—and these would be in Springfield, Ill., and not in Washington—his real operating center. He, too, would be essentially a coalition candidate, if an unsuccessful one, ready and willing to draw as far as possible away from a sitting Democratic President, Truman, who was a vestigial symbol of the *party* method of running politics. For Stevenson's activities and purposes, too, would be shaped by the new political realities.

These realities would be thus expressible: If you can't lick them (that is, this and that bloc of presumably hostile voters) persuade them to join you. A political phase would open out in which the authentic power would lie almost wholly not in party associations but in the sheerly personal ability to get elected to public office. The "Mr. Republican" of that period, Senator Robert A. Taft of Ohio, would be handsomely returned to the Senate in 1950, for example, not at all because of what he stood for and not at all because of organizational Republican efforts but because he was Taft *the person.*

Thus party structures, the old pyramidic forms in which the national committee stood proudly at the apex, would become hardly more than dying appendages to the new evolutionary politics. The Republican National Committee types would take all this with the philosophic calm which is more nearly characteristic of Republicans generally than of Democrats. But the Democratic National Committee types would enter upon a decade and more of a frantic unwillingness to lie down and die quietly.

These would continue, through the years, to struggle frantically in support of a proposition which was demonstrably untrue: that there still was a Democratic Party, in the old sense, and that the Democratic Party could win Presidential elections as the late *Roosevelt*-Democratic Party had done. They would become the most exasperating of all men in politics—the undue, the overlong, mourners of a man, Roosevelt, who had gone forever. Roosevelt had taught them too much and too little. His cheerful pragmatism would become their wretched and hopeless sentimentalism.

They would continue to act as though as a country we were still in the Thirties and early Forties; as though the now long-dead New Deal were still churning out its sometimes wild and always wonderful alphabetical agencies; and as though FDR were still in the White House addressing the nation in the fireside chat over a radio long since succeeded by a television screen, a new mechanism in a new time. Even Mrs. Eleanor Roosevelt would get a little weary, sometimes, of this vastly overlong half-wake, this extraordinary delusion that time had not passed. She would, for one instance, go privately before a group of Roosevelt idolators at the Democratic National Convention in 1956—eleven years after the funeral on that April day in the White House—to tell them with a brisk, firm kindness that we were not forever fixed in time and that 1945 was long in the past; that there were now new problems, new techniques and new men.

Still not all the rolling march of history—and not the overwhelming 1952 victory of Eisenhower or the even more overwhelming 1956 second victory of Eisenhower—would convince these national-committee types that things had changed. They would look at their organizational charts. They would linger over the undoubted fact (for what it was worth) that far more people were more-or-less Democratic than more-or-less Republican. Thus, after Election Day, they would demand of their private gods to know what had happened in this world to mathematics, and to simple justice.

We should see, in short, a steady deterioration of the position in fact of the forms of organized politics and, at the same time, a steady, continuous assertion by the old Democratic organizers of the dubious claims of a kind of politics which no longer had much substance except in their tireless memories.

Not in many other ways would the effect of Roosevelt's influence be more clearly illustrated. For while the whole nature of the Democratic struggle after his death would become altered beyond recognition, those who thought themselves the true heirs of his tradition would go on and on as though nothing at all had changed. In the new, somewhat equivocal and always loosely knit quasi-party structure that would follow him, these men would sustain a long and futile clamor which was intended to suggest that organizational Democratic politics remained a vibrant force.

Ineffectual Democratic National Chairman would succeed ineffectual Democratic National Chairman until, toward the end of the decade of the Fifties, the apogee of this form of backward looking would be reached. As has been seen, Stevenson himself—who would remain the Democratic hero from 1952 to the onset of 1960—would never be unaware that a new politics had come. He would invest no real power or confidence in the old national-committee concept. But men who among all the Roosevelt rememberers were the most desperately constant rememberers would take possession of what was left of the National Committee. And they would carry forward one of the silliest—and also the saddest—lost causes of modern politics.

Paul Butler of Indiana would most of all typify this Sancho Panza affair, as Democratic Chairman for a span of about eight years. The country would see a time in which the Democratic National Committee, superbly unperceiving of the vast difference between the Roosevelt and the post-Roosevelt years, would try to force the adoption of campaign techniques and issues which went into history on the day that the great man, Roosevelt, died.

In a country which was moving forward as rapidly in economic terms as it was sleepily resting in terms of thinking actively about political and foreign issues, the Democratic National Committee types would do—what? They would solemnly set up "advisory councils," made up for the most part of men who had served Democratic Administrations now only alive in memory, to "advise" a new Democratic politics which was bound to regard such admonitions for what they were: echoes from an honorable, but a quite finished, past.

The centrists of the party would be too busy with the present—and the future—to look overmuch into these recommendations from yesterday. Besides, the new masters of a party-that-had-been would be conditioned by a bedrock awareness that it was, indeed, a party-that-had-been and not a party that was.

They would rightly sense not only that there could be no going back to the party systems and methods of the pre-Roosevelt times. They would not only grasp the palpable truth that the public now regarded deep controversy and contention as bad form. They would not only comprehend that Competence had succeeded Command as the people's touchstone of what American politics should be and should achieve. They also would reckon that the requirement lying heaviest upon them, if they were to succeed as politicians, was to work and live always at the center; to flee always from fringe, whether far left or far right.

So it would turn out that Stevenson, though twice defeated by Eisenhower, would lose his preeminence among the Democrats not simply because of these defeats but actually more because of a fatal inability to push aside the enveloping and destructive affection for him of the sentimental rememberers who would not really accept it that Roosevelt was now dead. At the beginning of 1960 the position would be this: Four Democrats would be rational "possibilities" for the Presidential nomination that summer—Stevenson, Senators Stuart Symington of Missouri, John F. Kennedy of Massachusetts, Lyndon B. Johnson of Texas.

Stevenson, who would be seen in retrospect as one of the most singular victims of singular irony in the history of our politics, by rational standards would have been the most probable nominee. His twin failures before Eisenhower's massive popularity need not have been mortally damaging in themselves. For everybody had known that nobody could have beaten the American hero of the Second World War in a period when reaction from Roosevelt (and to a lesser extent from Truman) had been inevitable.

Moreover, Stevenson would be, of all the four possibilities, the one really most different from the Roosevelt mold and the Roosevelt time. He would be the man most inherently capable of expressing, of leading and of personifying the new politics of the middling middle way. He would be the man most truly aware of the pre-Roosevelt traditions. For he was, truly, the most conservative and traditional of the four—save, perhaps, for very partial exception of Johnson on the single issue of civil rights. But it would come about that the true Stevensonian ideological position could not be maintained even by Stevenson himself—because the rememberers for the most part would clutch and seize upon him as the model of their memories and the human vehicle for their hopeless dream of a return to yesterday. He would not be defeated for nomination in 1960 by his enemies or even by his temperate critics. He would be defeated not by his friends but rather by his idolators—and idolators who were really enchanted not with *him* but with a man then long dead with whom they persisted in identifying, with total irrationality, the man who was living.

Instead, the two most powerful of the centrists, Kennedy and Johnson, would fight it out—but in a contest which, again, would be far more over human and personal matters (geography, mainly) than over issues. They would contend not at all for the bankrupt relic of the Democratic national organization; they would contend, rather, for the right to lead the new centrism into the Sixties from new sources of personal power. Kennedy would win this battle with Johnson—but neither of them would win or lose a war over ideology. For they would be, in respect of nearly all great public ques-

tions, really very much alike—with Republican candidate
Nixon not much more than a stone's throw from either—in
that they both really would *know* the new politics of the ever-
expanding center.

True, Kennedy would allow the Democratic National Convention to write a platform of such "liberalism" as to make
the 1948 third party of Henry Wallace look a bit on the
cautious side. But this would be a sop to the old politics of
organization and of formal structure (in the old politics you
had to have a "platform committee" and so on, because you
were then dealing with organized, structural politics, old
style). But if Kennedy would permit the issuance of this
document it would also follow that Johnson—that presumed
symbol of conservatism—would stand wholly upon it also,
for the record. And, more important, Kennedy as a candidate
would run on a *Kennedy* platform, which most of all sought
accommodation, in the end, of every issue capable of being
accommodated in the sixth decade of this century. And, even
more significantly, he would run his own show—exactly as
would Nixon on the other side—with only the smallest of
formal bows to the national committee notion of a campaign.
The key, the essential, the real Kennedy advisers would be
within Kennedy's own direct, personal command and in direct, intimate association with him personally.

Chapter

Twenty-Two

Now the brief funeral service in the White House, the next to last act of our official national mourning for Franklin Roosevelt was drawing in cool, dry good taste to its close. For five minutes during the prayers for the dead there had been the first total national hiatus, of so much as a minute, from the hour when the Japanese bombs descending upon Pearl Harbor had thrust us into the war. For these five minutes every American military man all about the world, save for those immediately, personally and directly engaged in combat on one or another of the world's battle lines, had stood at ease and in silence, to offer, if he so chose, some petition of his own for the Commander in Chief who had, as many quite truly said, fallen in action. For those five minutes the immense war production machine—that machine which had been Roosevelt's most historic single contribution to an Allied victory that would be won strictly by mass of matériel and of maneuver—ground to a shuddering, an absolute halt across thousands of square miles of plants and mines and shipyards.

It was a curiously fitting thing that this great apparatus should thus participate, if in mindless and hulking inanimation, in the farewell to Franklin Delano Roosevelt. For it had been Roosevelt's incredible ability to gather up and whip up this country's material strengths and resources—"to turn out the stuff" had been the phrase used among us—which would be seen as his principal claim to be remembered in history for his wartime leadership. His notions of high strategy had not on the whole been very sound. His capacity for stating very lofty and shimmering postwar aims—the four freedoms, and all that—would later be seen to reflect more credit upon his decent intention than upon his grasp of the hard realities of world politics. But there was here as superb an irony as any of the many ironies that he had left us to ponder upon. This President, who had been so endlessly and so thoroughly detested by so large a part of the American business and industrial community, had been held alien by it largely because its leaders had always thought of him as a dilettante squire and a mere "politician" who not only had "never met a payroll" but was too dainty-fingered to have any notion of how one went about making things and moving them about in the market place.

But what had been the truth? It had turned out that Franklin D. Roosevelt, New Deal ideas and all, had been the greatest master of production and of the movement of production that the world had known. He had taken this country by the seat of its pants and sometimes by the scruff of its neck, and made it the "Arsenal of Democracy" in an even truer and vaster sense than that slogan could possibly indicate.

Once, at the onset of our own participation in the war, he had, in that airy way which so infuriated the businessman type, tossed off a remark that perhaps he would make fifty thousand aircraft within a year's space. Business had sourly scoffed at this as the most arrant nonsense of which even "that man" had yet been guilty. He had only grinned and gone ahead to make many more than fifty thousand planes a year—along with countless other weapons.

Here again—and almost as though their destruction had been a great part of his purpose on this earth—he had smashed cliché-images with a happy abandon. For he had been, this man over whose body Bishop Dun was now concluding the Office of the Dead, not really a liberal innovator, but rather a great conservator; not really a creator of ideology, but rather a maker of things; not really an intellectual but rather a doer. Had he chosen early in his life and with the same enthusiasm, to have become a captain of industry rather than a captain of public affairs, God knows how many payrolls he might have met; God knows what monoliths of trade and commerce he might have raised in the name of Roosevelt. The good Dutch-burgher men-of-affairs who had been in his background had not put their mercantile blood into him for nothing.

For this man had run an industrial enterprise a thousandfold greater than the combined operations back in the late Thirties of those members of the Liberty League who had looked so askance at his presumed ignorance in the matter of business and industry. What he had done for the war, beyond providing men, was to provide the *things*—the endless, inexhaustible line of machines and weapons which, flung in his myriads of cargo ships out across every sea and into the far deserts and islands and atolls, had broken Hitler and Tojo and their associates under a crushing weight which not all their combined war economies—stolen and indigenous—could begin to rival.

He had immensely simplified the problems of his field commanders—and measurably eased those of the relatively impoverished British and other allies—by an outpouring of the goods of war which had astonished his foreign friends along with his foes. His armies had marched on more than their stomachs; his fleets had floated to victory on more than seas of oil; his troops had been carried to inevitable victory, like small, insentient stones caught up in an avalanche of irresistible mass. His fighting men had been able to use and even waste weapons and vehicles, whether on or above or below the earth's surface, with a grand, sweeping prodigality that had to be seen to be believed by numbed allies and numbed enemies alike. (I still remember being touched by the wistful poverty of Marshal Bernard Montgomery's British forces in Normandy, in terms of weapons and supply and transport, relative to the unlimited resources at the disposal of General Omar Bradley, who could cast his divisions forward like the pebbles which he would sometimes drop from his hand as he briefed his subordinate commanders on his next offensive operations.)

So if Roosevelt was leaving us, on that afternoon of the funeral, with a new and unpretty materialism among the people, he was leaving us also with a true legend of incomparable value. The United States, under his leadership, had mastered the techniques of production—whether for peace or for war—as no other nation had ever done or was ever likely to do. There had been an industrial breakthrough which gave to this country an opportunity for an enduring primacy in this world no less significant than the primacy which long before had been given to Britain in the first of the West's series of industrial revolutions. We stood, at this hour, upon a pinnacle of industrial power and potential which was without example in all time; we stood upon the summit of a power to *make* things, to *move* things, to *command* things.

Surely, therefore, we would have no reason ever again to fear for the material base of our national life. In this regard we had, in the most explicit sense, no reason any longer to fear what Roosevelt had once so memorably called "fear itself."

There in the White House East Room on this April afternoon this thought perhaps had occurred to the President's widow. For Bishop Dun now approached the last-but-one of his funeral tasks as he uttered the final prayer:

O God, from Whom every good thing cometh, we thank Thee for the qualities of heart and mind which this Thy servant brought to the service of our nation and our world.

For steadfast courage in adversity; for clear vision of dangers to which they may shut their eyes; for sympathy with the hungers and fears of common men; for trials met without surrender, and weakness endured without defeat; for unyielding faith in the possibility of a more just and ordered world delivered from the ancient curse of war; we praise Thee, O God.

But now came the very last funeral salute, the one which Eleanor Roosevelt had asked the Bishop to make:

"In his first inaugural address the President bore testimony to his own deep faith; so, first of all, let me assert my own belief that 'the only thing we have to fear is fear itself.'

"As that was his first word to us, I am sure he would want it to be his last. We should go forward in the future as those who go forward without fear, without fear of our allies or friends, and without fear of our own insufficiencies."

After the Constitutional Convention, old Benjamin Franklin had told the early Americans that they had now got a Republic; time would tell whether they would deserve it and could keep it. Now Roosevelt had bequeathed to us a far less grand and a much less noble thing, an economically and industrially secure country from which it would on the whole be clearly possible to banish all genuine want, except for such of those as would be mentally or physically unable to grapple, even softly, with the now far softer demands of economic life.

But it would be very far from a little or an ignoble thing,

this bequest of a man who had been praised and damned in life for qualities he had never had (as in the widespread belief that he was a revolutionary theorist) and so little praised for the qualities which had actually been paramount in him (the inspired pragmatism with which he had filled the bellies and incomparably strengthened the economic muscle of the people).

I am no economist, but I think it reasonably exact to assert, from the vantage point of 1961, that Roosevelt had left this country, even granting the grave foreign-policy errors I have ascribed to him, inherently able to overcome every challenge of external and material danger that could in the foreseeable future be mounted by any other system. For what he had really done was to remake this country from a *good* to an *absolutely preeminent* industrial power, quite capable, if it really would go to work as he had put it to work, of smothering the industrial output of such as the Soviet Union.

How had he done this? By turning this country's capacity progressively to producing not necessarily the best, but the most; as indeed he had done during the war. By creating a political climate and a national mood (and a series of imbedded legislative acts) which consciously and totally would turn this from what in 1932 had still been a quasi-agrarian society to a strictly big-industry society. We had become not merely a corporate, but also a corporation, society—from the very day, actually, that the concept of the NRA Blue Eagle had gone into the national consciousness and into national practice. And if there would now be far less room for unemployment, and none for outright depression, there would also be progressively far less room for small business, for small enterprise of any and every kind.

This circumstance in itself would have much to do with making this more a welded people. For apartness prospers in a certain degree of isolation or comparative isolation. The three small grocers in the town will maintain more separation than the three clerks who will work—and curse—together in the successor chain-store establishment which comes in to take all the grocery business and so drives out the crustily inefficient but somehow appealing old boys who used to run the dusty, outmoded little separate shops and welcome or run away their customers as cantankerous spirit might move them.

Chapter

Twenty-Three

So, some would speak of the Managerial Revolution which had been caused by or—depending on the point of view—merely had coincided with the time of Roosevelt. A Managerial Revolution there certainly was and would be; but it was and would be perhaps not quite the kind they had in mind. Roosevelt had been, in *himself*, a Managerial Revolution of lasting significance. For he had, in his own personality and in his own personal actions, made an extraordinary marriage of convenience, between politics and business, of a wholly new kind. The old association had been an illicit liaison. It had been one in which the one partner, Big Business, was a fat and evil old chap handing clandestine money to the other partner, the Politician, for doing things in favor of Business and against the people.

In a word, this had been a liaison in which there was neither much joy nor much reluctance among the parties to it, as there was no opportunity for true growth within either. But the new marriage was one in which the one partner, Business, had been dragged, screaming imprecations, to the altar. There was not simply reluctance here; there was bitter resistance. Politician, however, remained calmly unmoved by these hostile lamentations. For Politician knew that he must manage Business (as Roosevelt for years actually had done, in the higher sense if not in the mere details) as a means of managing the country and as a means of enabling Business, in the end, so to conduct itself as to secure the country's industry and economy.

Now this would be for a time a most uncomfortable honeymoon; an imperceptive onlooker would have supposed from the long violence of Business's language that Politician was committing upon Business such outrages as ought to be kept from the public prints and not really mentioned even in polite private society. But all this was only the superficial aspect. To drop the marital metaphor, Roosevelt's association with business would be seen, in the deepest sense, one to help business to help itself. Now, he would never be liked, even in memory and in retrospect, by Business with a capital B; for it would be necessary to sustain the folk image of the more or less "socialistic" President who had fallen like a ravening wolf upon free enterprise. But this, fundamentally, would be only rubbish. One would be able to look back from the later years and to assert with some confidence the following proposition: There never had been any rational reason for business *generally* to be either alarmed by or hostile to Roosevelt. On the contrary, business *generally* would have real cause to do what its self-inflicted and purely psychosomatic traumas would never permit it to do—to thank the big man for what he had done for it. The only part of business that ever had any logical reason to oppose Roosevelt at every turn was made up of the *owners* of business. There had always been a certain common sense, if a somewhat limited common sense, in their views; after all, these had been the men who had to pay the taxes Roosevelt had laid upon them. (Even these taxes would look far less onerous later on.) But these owners, even in Roosevelt's time, had been numerically, and even in operating influence, only a small part of business generally. The great majority of operating business would become, more and more, its paid managers rather than its owners. And these fellows would find their affairs, more and more, inextricably mixed with those of government—Truman's government and Eisenhower's government no less than Roosevelt's government.

They would find, too (though they never would admit it as to Roosevelt's government), not only that "Washington" was an irreplaceable part of their business lives but that "Washington" would become more and more their best and most indispensable customer. (Remember the Marshall Plan; remember defense orders.) If Roosevelt had been able to persuade no more than a tiny handful of big-business men to enter the mysteries of the national bureaucracy, the following years would find the tycoons entering these supposedly evil and hostile labyrinths in increasing numbers—Democratic as well as Republican. Even so perfectly dreadful a President as Truman (from the point of view of the old folklore of Business) would obtain some of his ablest—and most co-operative—administrative assistants from the citadel of Wall Street itself. The most distinguished of them, Robert A. Lovett, would have many companions from those rich canyons—and he would in time head the list of the new industrial statesmen who were to be born, so to speak, from that new marriage of Politician and Business of which I spoke a while back.

And if the old-time owners of business, the vanishing class of individual proprietors, had had at least a little reason to sustain an enmity toward Roosevelt, the managers of business would find that they had had no such reason in the first place and that they could not rationally sustain such enmity in the second place. It would have been irrational and irrelevant —as though the production superintendent of a textile mill in North Carolina, which was beyond doubt a part of the old

Confederacy, had refused to ship his finished cloths north to New York because he didn't like the fact that Sherman had got away with that march to the sea.

For Roosevelt had mixed and mingled, forever and in a new sense, the affairs of business with the affairs of government—which is to say of politics. The great new national labor unions were now facts of life, no longer mere nightmare fears. They had to be dealt with; and in them, too, would rise a new managerial class who would become, as individuals, less and less distinguishable from the pristine managerial class of business. With the arrival of the corporation state it would become quite impossible—not to say quite irresponsible—to refuse to deal with those who would become indispensable parts as labor managers of that state, as surely as the minority was, along with the majority, an indispensable part of the political state.

A great and novel objectivity—and a degree of mutual toleration—would come into the national life as between the men of business and the practitioners of politics, all resulting from what had once been thought to have been the profound antibusiness subjectivity of Roosevelt. This movement, partly one of outright merger of business and politics and partly one of shifting business attitude toward politics, would have a tremendous impact on the old, heretofore rather stratified, party structures now crumbling away. It would, for illustration, soon become not only possible but fairly common for very rich men of industry to make long-term or short-term alliances even with politicians who in some ways were not merely open Democrats but held some views which the folklore of business had always declared to be heretical in the extreme. Roosevelt's brilliant wartime lend-lease concept had necessarily intermingled the affairs of business with world politics (while enormously adding to the profits of business).

Businessmen had even earlier been taken out of their offices and away from their charts for small, fugitive glimpses of the unavoidable new interrelationship betwixt business as no longer a wholly private function and politics as no longer a tricky, double-dealing, secret art from which all sound capitalistic types should naturally flee as from a trollop archly patrolling the public streets in the nighttime. This much the old code days of the NRA—which really amounted to a license to business to forget the restraints of the antitrust laws if only it would hire more hands from the relief rolls—had accomplished. If it had not made politics actually respectable in the eyes of business it had empirically convinced business that politics really was here to stay and that even that allegedly nonpolitical thing called commerce would now and henceforth have to coexist with the politicians.

And then, as the war was closing coincidentally with the life of Roosevelt, there would be further grand developments which would continue to mix and mingle the affairs, the prospects and even the functioning of business with those of politics. It would shortly be found that just as lend-lease had been necessary to help win the war it would become necessary to have a successor to lend-lease. This would be required not merely in common decency; for much of the terrain of ancient allied lands lay in a shambles of human and economic death. It would also be required for the economic safety and progress of this nation itself. Thus would come about the Marshall Plan. This would be the supreme expression of that alliance of necessity between politics and business upon which Roosevelt had set out, in a small, tentative way so long ago, in NRA and in the other alphabetical policies which while often seeming to business to be punitively directed against business had in fact been directed to the salvation of business.

True, the Marshall Plan would be formalized some time

after Roosevelt's departure from this earth. True, it could not, in the literal sense, be called his invention. It would be, however, the logically inevitable extension of his economic policies, and with a strong touch of that tough pragmatism which had so characterized so much of what he had done. For the Marshall Plan would most pragmatically be prepared not by the politicians (though lend-lease had been prepared by them) but by the men of business themselves. Its true authors would be businessmen such as Will Clayton of Texas, the very model of the great free enterprisers as head of the world's largest firm of cotton factors.

These men would move in ways and for purposes sufficiently realistic to please the most hardheaded capitalist who ever lived. They themselves would, of course, be motivated by a genuine concern for the ravaged continent of Europe. (And in the process it would be borne in upon them and upon their business associates nearly everywhere that politicians—even Democratic politicians—could be motivated decently, too.) But most of all they would be impelled by plain, unromantic realities: The war had ended; the vast industrial plant of the United States—and the swellingly productive farm lands which had long been tilled at forced draft to help feed so many millions in so many lands—would now require new outlets and markets to replace the old; Europe had for generations been our great overseas market; again, the customer would have to be served.

Here, for the first time in our history, a great political policy, one of a happy blending of enlightened self-interest and plain mercantile interest, had been thought up and implemented by men of business working in tandem with the politicians.

True, the policy had been named not for a great businessman but for a great general, George C. Marshall. But Marshall himself had been the first to disclaim the act of creation; he had been well and wryly aware from the first that the credit line had gone to him because of his famous name. (And, oddly, he would never hold that plan in quite so high an esteem as would the business types who really made it in co-operation with politicians like Dean Acheson. Once recalling to the general in his retirement some of the marks of his famous career, I remarked: "I suppose the high point for you was your service as Secretary of State and your sponsorship of the Marshall Plan." He looked at me in cold unbelief and replied: "Good God, don't you realize that I spent forty years in the *United States Army?*" For him, the apex of his life had not been his work as a Cabinet officer but rather as Chief of Staff of that "United States Army.")

But the main point of the moment is that the genially and mutually erosive effects of the long encounters between the men of business and the men of politics in making the Marshall Plan would long outlast even that superb example of a rational high politics in action. In matters of this kind—in every aspect of foreign and defense policies, as illustrations— the partisan label of the participant would become less and less relevant. The great turn to a political and economic internationalism which had been forced upon Roosevelt by the intractable realities posed by Hitler and Company had of necessity brought into active politics (even into Roosevelt politics) a whole class, that of business and industry, whose association with that art had theretofore been more one of a reluctant and condescending patronage than an aware participation.

Now these men would enter politics, in ever-increasing numbers and thus with ever-widening spheres of influence, in a spirit that would tend to reject the old clear-cut partisan images. Naturally, they would bring with them into politics the kind of assistants, and the administrative and persuasive techniques, which they had found useful at home—whether in the factory or in the Wall Street investment and banking house.

To be sure, these business managers now to become so active in politics would tend mostly to a vaguely Republican partisanship—in the sense, at least, that very few would admit to be card-carrying Democrats. But it would be demonstrated over and over again that they had none of that emotional and romantic attachment to Republicanism as such, whether old-style or new-style, which to the old class of vehemently anti-Roosevelt businessmen had been as right and as inevitable an attachment as was that, say, to the Union League Club, the Manufacturers Association or the Episcopal Church—which they had so uncomfortably shared with that traitor to his class, Franklin Roosevelt.

For the business managers in politics would find their true interest not so much in parties as in the impersonal and visible economic issues of the times—how, for instance, to use tariff concessions to promote necessary reciprocal foreign trade, without exposing domestic enterprise to ruinous competition.

Chapter

Twenty-Four

Sometimes they would even find, and not greatly flinch from the odd discovery, that such and such a Democratic politician had actually a better notion of how to accomplish a thing like this than did his Republican opponent. For the most part, however, they would not be required to accept such apostasy. Instead they would simply spend what was required in money, in thought and in effort to develop and support political leaders willing to *call themselves* Republicans, but also intellectually committed to the new business-influenced politics of modified and essentially bipartisan conservatism. They would set out from what had been once, but was no more, a base of a traditional allegiance and move leftward until at length they would meet the new strictly political leaders who, moving rightward from where Roosevelt had left affairs, would fetch up at the political center.

The businessmen-politicians, like the unhyphenated politicians, had learned more from Roosevelt than he could ever have dreamed they would learn and more than they would ever be aware they had learned: *expertise, getting the job done, and never mind too much about the old political forms and structures, and all that.* These lessons would be followed in some ways by much oversimplification. Where he had acted, in building a Roosevelt-Democratic Party, without conscious purpose to break up the old party but only to effectuate his current designs in the quickest possible way, the new business-men-in-politics would from the very start be largely free of even a sentimental remembrance of any personal partisan commitment. (Recall that even in the old politics these managerial men had never been "married" to the G.O.P.; the association at most had been a rather furtive liaison.) And though for the most part they would not ever formally leave what was now left of the Republican Party, post-Roosevelt, in its old context and tone, they would become in fact men not of attachment to partisan forms and instrumentalities but rather men of attachment to empirical political action. If the results they sought could be had from politicians calling themselves Republican, so much the better; but in the end their whole drive would be simply for the *results*.

Thus, by rich japery of fate, it would be seen that the one President most distrusted by business had caused businessmen not only to enter politics as they had never done before, but to enter with no strengthening whatever of the party which traditionally had been supposed to "speak for business."

It would come about that the Republican Party, after Roosevelt's death, would make one final stab at nominating a more-or-less Republican for President, Thomas E. Dewey. After that, in 1952 and again in 1956, it would choose a man who was neither a Republican nor a Democrat, but instead a perfect symbol of the mingling of business and politics, General Eisenhower. The efforts of the business and industrial community for General Eisenhower in the election of 1952 would become instantly and widely known and apparent. But the truly vital function of this community would be discharged long before the election and would not generally be understood at all. This function would be the destruction of the last—if then still strong—remnants of traditional, organized, structural Republicanism. For the men of business now active in politics would take a fundamental decision, many months before the Republican convention of 1952, amounting to a final acceptance of the new and essentially unpartisan politics. This decision was that the only truly Republican figure of established national stature in contention for the Presidency, Senator Robert A. Taft of Ohio, must on no account be allowed to have it.

Though by any criterion known to the old politics Taft had earned, and triply earned, the designation as a uniquely powerful and passionate partisan of his party, the consensus would be that precisely for that reason he must not be allowed the nomination. What would be sought, and what would be found, instead was a nominee fitting perfectly into the new politics without abrasion (or without tears) and into the new concept of the achievement of national and political goals through more or less Republican personages whose skill lay in accommodation and in a kind of antiseptic amiability. This personage, of course, would be Mr. Eisenhower.

When 1960 came around, the problem would appear at first glance to be a more difficult one—that the new businessman-politician controllers of the center would be forced, in the person of Richard Nixon, to reverse the movement of the new politics and take a nominee from the slim surviving ranks of the anachronistic G.O.P. This, however, would be seen, if one looked a bit below the surface, to be only superficially true. For Nixon in fact would be one of the most dramatic possible personal illustrations of how far the new politics had moved.

His career in national politics would open, just after Roosevelt's death, in the twilight hours of the old politics which pitted partisan organization against partisan organization. But it also would open—in his election to Congress from California—

in circumstances wherein Nixon himself had not been too
sure, only a little time beforehand, whether he was a Republican or a Democrat.

And a series of accidents—notably his participation in the
Congressional investigations which would lead early in that
career to the Alger Hiss scandal and the accompanying great
hunt for "Communists in government"—would seem for a
time to place him as an authentic, if outdated, old-school Republican. This, however, would turn out to be a case where
art, the fortuities and opportunities of the time, would for a
space overcome nature—Nixon's inherent position as a practitioner of the new politics of performance above partisanship,
of achievement by way of coalitions formed at the ever-
expanding political center of American life.

Roosevelt's acts and policies as a highly personal President
would be seen to have largely contributed to killing what he
had used very much, the American institution of the party
form as the erstwhile dominant factor in working politics.
What an incredible state of affairs would unfold! Roosevelt
had raised up a quasi-Democratic coalition designed really
only to achieve programs which were ideological in meaning
only in the minds of those followers who had wrongly thought
Roosevelt to be an earnest ideologue, whereas he had been
in fact as practical in his purpose as any manufacturer. And
this quasi-Democratic coalition would now be succeeded, in
both parties, by centrist coalitions also designed only to
achieve. These new coalitions would pay much less attention to party labels than he had really paid. They would
not even pretend to give much room to ideological debates
—the kind of debate which had actually bored him but which
he had found useful to his immediate purposes in a country
far less sophisticated politically when he had come to power
than when he had laid that power down in death.

And as, for good or for ill, he had caused the actual and responsible and enduring involvement of men of affairs in politics, so he had brought the intellectuals truly and deeply, and for the first time, into the country's genuine political life. Here they would long remain. The intellectuals, mainly from the academic world, had begun in the first months of the first Roosevelt Administration to emerge blinking from their classrooms to take a direct hand in politics—mostly bureaucratic politics at first; for at first they had flinched from those who are the real politicians, the elected types. This was a new generation of intellectuals, on what was to it—and to every other generation of intellectuals—an entirely new mission. A few men in an earlier professorial generation had dabbled briefly and unsuccessfully at the fringes of the kind of politics which Woodrow Wilson had brought from Princeton, by way of the governorship of New Jersey, to the White House. But the times had been out of joint then for this kind of intellectual participation; Wilson's New Freedom had been a far cry from Roosevelt's New Deal. For Wilson was not a good politician and Roosevelt was the best we had ever known—or would soon know again.

If the Roosevelt era had brought about a marriage between business and politics, it had also brought about a most curious relationship between politics and the intellectuals. The businessmen—even those avant-garde businessmen who had early got into politics—had entered the affair with a certain cool skepticism which would endure. They had decided that this was the clearly indicated means for what was plainly and simply indispensable to them, a coexistence with politics. But the intellectuals had got mixed up with politics, as the saying used to go, with far less simple motives and far more complicated emotional attitudes. They had not gone in first and foremost to forward their own personal or professional interests. They were not there to coexist but rather to cooperate, in the making of history and of reform, with a man, Roosevelt, toward whom they had been markedly cool until, subsequent to his nomination, he had thrown overboard a profoundly conservative platform in favor of the bold innovations of the First Hundred Days of the New Deal.

Before the nominating convention of 1932 most of them had thought of Roosevelt—and they were quite right at that time—as an engaging man, gallant in recovering from the paralysis of polio, whose early political career had been largely not on his own power but rather as the gift of the gods and of an inherited family name. They had known quite well that here was no giant, creative, liberal intellect. (In this they were surely right; though they were, later on, quite to forget that the estimate of him they had had in this one connection in the first place had been right then and would remain right to the end.) The liberal intellectuals of the country, and particularly those in the East, had in fact been in the main anti-Roosevelt and pro-Al Smith before the 1932 convention—particularly since they had been aware that the Democratic Presidential nominee of 1932 was going to have to oppose a markedly liberal Republican for that time, in a man called Herbert Hoover. (What price the tags and slogans of yesteryear?)

So the intellectuals, though they would be prepared to join in the Roosevelt politics a good deal ahead of the plunge that would be taken by the businessmen types, had not at first gladly leapt into the Roosevelt era. When at length they would so leap they would make a good job of it; but they would find a very strange kind of association with him.

To it they would bring much that was useful—many ideas for social and economic justice (along with some surpassingly poor ones) and many dreams for a better and brighter national future. They would come to color some of Roosevelt's thinking, but far more they would color the public's impression of Roosevelt. They would persist from beginning to end in assuming that what he was about was reform toward a wholly new life—whereas what he was really about was rehabilitation of an old world to which, whenever he really thought deeply about it, he was greatly attached.

They would read too much into what he did and said. And, being scholars on the whole, they would assume the existence of a long-looking, a consistent and coherent logic of Roosevelt "planning." They would think he was playing from an elaborate score; he would really be playing by ear, in the irregular but inspired notes of the artist who operates by guess and by God far more than by the philosophic disciplines.

Chapter

Twenty-Five

There would be nothing very wrong in all this, and much that was right. True, there would be a rather bewildering number of mansions in the national House of Roosevelt. But there would be a richness and also a rough essential unity of diversities and pluralisms such as we had not known ever before. And there would be certain resulting untidinesses which would long remain with us. For the intellectuals would see Roosevelt's national purposes as much larger, more orderly, and more consistent than they really were, and would adopt as articles of faith certain political assumptions that never were true and never would be.

They would assume that the politics of protest which he had employed for certain purposes at certain times would be the enduring politics after he had gone and would dominate a party, the Democratic, which would in fact be not only wholly altered in form after he had gone but also wholly altered in its view of its own functioning, in its purposes and in its operating methods.

They would not concede the passage of time and the arrival upon the national scene of new circumstances in a new age and world. They would believe that the issues and the political approaches of the Thirties and early Forties would remain constants, even though the man now dead who had made those issues and those approaches had himself been moving away from them long before he died. They would therefore present the national political community with a sustained—and an embarrassing—political solecism. With some of the consequences of this situation I have already dealt; what is now in hand is an examination of some others.

Speaking broadly, it may be said Roosevelt had recruited into politics two estates which had previously had little to do with politics—except on the ideological fringes, as to the intellectuals, and in a usually rather surreptitious and cash-contribution way, as to the businessmen. Now, these two estates had opened during Roosevelt's life, and would long sustain after his death, a rivalry for possession of the mind and the purposes of the politics of the post-Roosevelt era.

This intramural contest between the two factions lately come into public life would persistently exhibit itself in both parties, though mainly in the Democratic, to a conclusion which can surely be regarded as foregone—though yet not even now wholly arrived at. That conclusion is that the business group (I speak here not of the old owning class but of its employed and objectively skilled administrators and spokesmen) would inevitably wind up winning this game. For, as I have rather suggested before this, Roosevelt as the Master Artist of politics had nevertheless killed its old art forms in mortally wounding the traditional party systems, with their collective action and collective determination of issues.

In largely supplanting collective party responsibility and action with intuitive personal responsibility and action in the Presidency he had done other things of great significance: He had opened the way for a true participation in politics (again, mainly Democratic politics) of these two classes, the academicians and the men of business, which for wholly dissimilar reasons had never been at home in the old structural, party politics. The academics had been essentially alien to this old politics for reasons of taste and conviction: As a class they could not long abide its somewhat crude "boss" aspects. And they could not fit—either comfortably or usefully—into a system which was more interested simply in controlling and getting out the vote than in preparing and discussing large, general issues of public affairs. The men of business, for their part, had not been so much repelled by the old politics—not even the old Democratic big-city machine politics—as they had found it simply too disorganized for their taste. They were much less readily suspicious of the motives of beings not within their normal paths of life, the politicians, than were the academics. But they just did not believe that these odd, rather shiftless, beings had a degree of competence justifying a true association with them.

So, Roosevelt had made it emotionally possible for the intellectuals to seize themselves of politics as a continuing interest. And he had made it rationally possible and—more important—rationally *necessary* for the business administrators, the Brain Trusters of Wall Street and Detroit.

But now that these two groups had been brought into the game on a continuing and serious basis, what would next follow? Roosevelt's unexampled success in the mercantilization of the country had also in a sense mercantilized its politics. What would be most urgently needed, in the political system post-FDR, would be largely the qualities exemplified by the business group, and only secondarily those exemplified by the academics.

Wherever any enterprise requires, simultaneously, the efforts of what are called "idea men" and the efforts of what are called administrators or managers, only the very naïve can be in much doubt as to which class will shortly come out on top. (A newspaper publisher friend once told me that of his two sons the younger was editor of his publications and was the brighter, but the older was paid a good deal more as his business manager. "But why?" I asked. "My friend," he replied with a smile, "ask me not why. This is just the way things are; the older son sits at the heart of this business, make no mistake about that.")

So it was that here, too, the business group would turn out to be the elder son—and the more influential one—among these recruits to the new politics. The whole style of politics would, in consequence, change enormously within a space of a dozen years beyond that day of the funeral parade of FDR. The business people, whose forte is always in merging and blending and managing the talents of those in subordinate association with them, would produce an entirely new picture of the proper national politician. He would become, in both parties, a man who shunned, rather than created, flamboyancies; a man of composite rather than striking personality —suggesting calm, competence, poise, order, dignity; usually a rather sophisticated kind of humor and of human style, as would be the case in 1960, for illustration, of every major aspirant for the Presidency in either party.

He would be a man never seen, so to speak, in that wide, theatrical cape which FDR had often worn. He would be a man, so to say, in a Brooks Brothers suit, whether he was from Massachusetts (Kennedy), from Texas (Johnson), from Missouri (Symington)—or from California (Nixon).

This would not mean at all that he was only a dull, conformist chap. It would only mean that he would reflect with reasonable faithfulness, in detail as well as in principle, the new image of a politics which had been so heavily and successfully infiltrated by the two recruits, Business and Academy.

(The word "image," by the way, would become one of

the most overworked in our national language, a term first brought forward by the intellectual and in due course put by the business man to work—and work and work.)

This somewhat uneasy collaboration in politics of businessmen and intellectuals would produce, beyond the mere surface descriptions thus far indicated, essentially this kind of national politician: He would be a man in three parts. At the core of his talent would remain the traditional skills of the traditional politician, persuasiveness, articulateness, great courage (yes, *courage*)—plus a new awareness of and a new involvement in the skills of the business administrator (good management) and the academician (the ability to make reasonably disinterested inquiry as a prerequisite to ultimately sound decisions).

In a word, the new politician would not—and could not—shun the businessman as simply a regrettably greedy and myopic type. Nor would he flee in terror from the intellectual as only a troublesome "professor" likely at any moment to put God knows what chaotic and ill-considered notions into politics. For it would turn out that the business administrator, as the dominant figure in the business-academic political twosome, would himself calm down the intellectual so that he could work readily in the new political climate. And the politician himself, standing at the apex of this triangle, would in his own way and time exercise the same kind of controlling influence over the business type.

The man to be elected President in 1960, John Fitzgerald Kennedy, would thus be a perfect type-figure of the new politician rising from the new politics of the time after Roosevelt. For in Kennedy would be found a perfect blending of twin abilities: to make use of the modern type of business administrator without falling under the control of business itself; and to make use of the academician without letting

the academician get out of hand in the highly practical ultimate function of politics, which is governance.

Businessman and intellectual, in the meantime, would, in a
mutually erosive process greatly assisted by external factors,
become to some extent more alike—or, rather, less and less
unlike. What might be called the era of public studies would
open out for the nation, largely through the development
of huge foundations by our erstwhile royal families of business and industry, the Rockefellers, the Fords and the like.

These would not only be enormously useful in fields running from the fostering of indigenous cultures to research
upon cancer; they would also have an increasingly weighty
effect upon the new politics in whose climate they had been
born. A peculiarly new kind of quasi-public man, the half-
intellectual, half-administrator to be produced within these
foundations, would rise with ever-increasing influence—again,
in both parties.

The reports of large and costly and exhaustive researches
made by these foundations into public affairs would become
the raw materials for politicians in many ways—and sometimes the source materials *of* politicians. Nelson Rockefeller,
for an example, would reach national stature largely on the
impulse of such studies made by and for the Rockefeller
brothers even before he had reached regional stature by becoming Governor of New York.

And the staffmen of the foundations would become largely
indistinguishable, except on nonessentials like the origins of
their salaries, from the new sets of staffmen to politicians—
in the state houses, in Congress, at the White House—who
would become necessary to the new politics.

In all these ways and more would the new estates in politics,
those of the businessman and the academician, become in-
separable parts of politics. Could all this be ascribed to what

Roosevelt had done and not done in his own oddly brilliant political career—a career which had surely cast into the national pond more rocks of more kinds to more mixed consequences than had any other political tenure or movement in our history? No one would argue, of course, that this was totally and without qualification a case of simple and exclusive cause and effect. But no one could seriously deny that there were demonstrably consequential effects; and that there was some clear causative connection between the way in which he had mastered the old art all too well and the development of the new art form—an art form tending to deny personalism and to promote a corporation type of politics—which now would arise in its place.

Chapter

Twenty-Six

Now it is time to look backward again, for the last time to the last yesterday—that yesterday on which Franklin D. Roosevelt's body would be placed in a grave upon a windy hill above the Hudson River. All his life he had loved rivers —this one, of course, most of all—with that full riverman's awareness that here was a force of benign soothing beauty but also of a savage, erosive, destructive power. All the great rivers of this country, from the Housatonic in New England to those which, far away, flow into the Pacific, had concerned him. His true conservationist heart had put the river into his hierarchy of special values, along with the tree. Do you remember, now, the series on the rivers of America which FDR personally—amidst all that he had had to do at that time—had arranged to be written, back in the darkest of all the dark days of the Great Depression as a part of the Works Progress Administration (WPA) Writers Project?

The river, with its suggestion of timeless continuity, its oddly apt reflection of the continental nature of Roosevelt's land, its depiction of homeness, had been one of the two greatest of the symbols which more than any other had always stirred the gusty sentiment in this gusty American squire, this carer for the home land. He had often liked, in his moods of mellowness over the Holland gin, to sing of home in a loud, eager baritone. Similes dealing with the river

—"crossing the river," "resting at the river's bank," "one more river to cross"—these and many other echoes of a peculiarly American folklore had touched him always, and comforted him frequently, in his long time of many troubles, in his long time of happy jousting with all those men and all those forces which had, here or there, on this issue or in that crisis, stood in his gayly imperious way.

God, one thought, what a *man* he had been, this essentially patriarchal, this paterfamilias gentleman whose supposed modernity of political thought had so lightly overlain (and so superficially indicated) the real, deeply traditional, character which had lain so solidly beneath. What had he not done, for home and the river—"Home" as a representative term for the land and the people he had saved at such great cost in so many terms and in so many ways; the "river" as a representative term for the swift movement of a truer union among the people which, again at many costs in many ways, he had set agoing!

On this day, Sunday, the fifteenth of April in 1945 at Hyde Park, New York, where they were preparing to bury Franklin Delano Roosevelt amongst the graves of his own people, so many monuments stood, now long familiar to the nation's people, in so many places about a wide, wide land. Had it been, a decade before, really only "leaf-raking," as so many critics had said so long and so loudly, when he had put the shuffling newly employed men to work from Seattle to San Antonio? There had been PWA (Public Works Administration); there had been CWA (Civil Works Administration); and there had been, always and always, so it had once seemed, WPA.

All these bureaucratic-sounding agencies, on this day of his burial, had themselves long since been buried and forgotten, obsolete memories of an emergent era long finished.

But the works they had done—some had been silly, of course —these yet remained. A great, shining beach for the people near the City of New York—Jones Beach, was it not called? Firehouses, public buildings of all kinds; these now stood in many towns and cities—and even a good many schoolhouses, too, though already these were becoming dingy-looking and "overcrowded," that ugly, dreary term which would, by the time the Sixties arrived, become a kind of gasping slogan to parents, to educators, to politicians alike.

From coast to coast there yet remained all these monu-ments (fittingly practical and pragmatic monuments to a leader of a kind of illuminated pragmatism). And there were many other monuments (millions of them, if it came to that) of another, a wholly human, kind. Not many families, on this fifteenth of April, 1945, had been untouched, in one member or another or through one relative or another, by what Roose-velt had done to *put the people back to work.*

(The old Negro spiritual—and this, too, Franklin Roose-velt in life had liked—had expressed it in not too dissimilar a way: "Let my people go.")

The unemployed had, at first, been only shuffling at this new work; for many had lost the sense of useful employment in its long denial to them. The unemployed had now, long since, become the usefully, the skillfully, the regularly em-ployed. But they could still remember. And now, all over this nation, they were remembering, not a great man who had made many great mistakes but a kind man who had gallantly and effectively *cared* and so acted to lift the nightmare of the early, the hopeless, the traumatic early Thirties.

So in this sense it could be said, without sentimentalism or archly pretty fancy, that millions were standing in spirit in the little village of Hyde Park with all its small, mannered beauty of the early springtime.

The skies in Hyde Park were very bright that Sunday morning; only the town hall threw off a note of conscious gloom, from its purple and black draperies. The funeral train had set off the night before at ten o'clock from Washington, four servicemen standing, as earlier they had stood from Warm Springs to Washington, at the corners of the coffin lying under the flag.

But, here too, as it had been in Washington, the whole tone and note was one of quietness in farewell. The train was switched away from the main tracks and onto a spur running alongside the Roosevelt estate, not through the streets of the town but rather up a country lane already showing the buds of early bloom. The coffin was carried through lines of decorated marines and soldiers, men home early from far battles in the far places of earth.

The twenty-one-gun salute rolled out; the muffled drums fell into the *thump, thump, thump* of the "Funeral March" while the young men of the West Point band turned their instruments just slightly toward the sky above. So up the lane slowly came this last of all the parades, the cadets marching three abreast, then the seven horses drawing the caisson, then a Negro trooper at the head of a riderless horse, the horse covered all in black and carrying a saddle with stirrups turned upward.

The coffin was now carried to the graveside and the band played "Nearer My God to Thee." Overhead, the airplanes— a handful among the uncounted tens of thousands which Roosevelt the doer and producer had made—wheeled and turned, so that at times it was difficult to hear the soft, kind words being softly uttered by Dr. George W. Anthony.

This, the rector of St. James's at Hyde Park, where Roosevelt had so long been senior warden, now had in his charge the last Office of all.

Unto Almighty God we commend the soul of our brother departed, and we commit this body to the ground; earth to earth, ashes to ashes and dust to dust, in sure and certain hope of the Resurrection unto eternal life; through our Lord Jesus Christ, at Whose coming in glorious majesty to judge the world, the earth and the sea shall give up their dead and the corruptible bodies of those who sleep in Him shall be changed and made like His glorious body, according to the Almighty whereby He is able to subdue all things to Himself.

Our Father which art in heaven, Hallowed be thy Name. Thy Kingdom come. Thy will be done in earth as it is in heaven. Give us this day our daily bread. And forgive us our debts as we forgive our debtors. And lead us not into temptation, but deliver us from evil: Amen.

So the body was now lowered into the grave and Dr. Anthony three times repeated, in the still air, the last verse of an old hymn—"Father, in Thy gracious keeping leave we now Thy servant sleeping."

The rifle salute blasted out over the closed grave; and Fala, the dead President's little dog, three times barked amid the sound of the guns.

Upon this place of burial at Hyde Park there fell then a great stillness—a stillness which for the many years to come would be only softly and occasionally disturbed by the visitors, mostly reverent visitors, who would come here to look upon the grave and to recall the years that had gone from all but memory.

But out across the world from which Roosevelt had forever departed the quietness of this scene was replaced by an extreme of violent sound and movement in many, many places about the world. The long spasms of the war were drawing now, in a last series of utter convulsions, to the end.

Roosevelt's great armies—those armies so soon to be of so

little use and to be allowed to crumble away—were driving forward for the kill in Europe, along with the massive and murderously effective Soviet legions of Stalin. The Russians were less than thirty miles from Berlin; the troops of Omar Bradley, of George Patton, of Courtney Hodges, and of Miles Dempsey and Bernard Montgomery of Britain were rolling eastward to invest a vast area radiating out from Czechoslovakia. An American-Russian troop juncture was near at hand.

The Nazis were now in that doomed mood of a grotesque frenzy of fear which, at every great crossroad of their defeat earlier in the war, they had shown. But this time their fear was at the highest pitch of psychotic madness; Hitler in Berlin and his principal accomplices were now preparing a gross travesty of a Wagnerian opera-melodrama of suicide and murder.

How strange it was that a small, single mound of new-turned earth, in a little place in America called Hyde Park, now represented all that remained of what had been, until short days beforehand, the greatest personification of power in all the world.

For soon, in a single city—Berlin—in a single one of the war's vast theaters, the dead would lie so high, amidst the most ghastly rubble up to then ever dreamed of by mankind, as almost to blot out earth-level vision, a dreadful fog of death which, to any sensitive postwar visitor, for years later would still hang above that city. How far would it be—how many millions of miles and how many eons of time in the moral and spiritual sense—between that small quiet grave in a garden above the Hudson and that indescribably horrible mausoleum of acre upon acre of blood-red and menacing granite which, in divided Berlin, the Russians would later raise up and choose to call their "Garden of Remembrance?"

And how good it was that since death had come for the

President it had come before he could learn of the infinite savageries which were to be worked in Berlin between the two maniacal and all but devil-possessed forces, the "liberating" invaders, the Russians, whom Roosevelt's policies had allowed to be first into Berlin, and the crazed Nazi defenders wallowing in such an evil blood lust as not even Genghis Khan himself had known.

Woodrow Wilson, a generation before, had not "saved the world for democracy," because no man could, and only time and the blind interplay of immense and complicated forces could tell whether any number of men ever really could.

Just so, Franklin Delano Roosevelt in helping to cleanse the world of the one dreadful scourge, fascism, had not saved that world from the consequences—some of them evil consequences which his own shortsightedness had surely done much unconsciously to promote.

Still we had had in this fallen President a man and not a god; a creature of warmth, and also therefore of error; an occupant of the high Presidential office upon whom had fallen the necessity to meet as best he could, at the time, the endlessly marching line of crises which had beset both nation and world.

Mistakes and mischief he had made, and some of them ghastly. But charity and warmth and generosity he had served —and, as he himself had once recalled, the divine Dante himself had reckoned that the sins of the warm-blooded and the cold-blooded are rightly weighed up in different scales.

So the summing-up: I have not set out here upon any mean little, meaching little, bookkeeper's enterprise of balancing every sheet of the books at all cost; just so much to Credit, just so much to Blame; just so much to Maybe and so much to Perhaps and If Only. I am raising as best I can a salute to the memory of a great but humanly marred man and Man of Politics; an earned salute, an honest salute; a critically informed salute; not a stick of sugar candy handed out to those who blindly adored, and not a contribution of malice to those who blindly hated.

Let those who love without thought go on loving; but let them know that the man they have in mind would never have cared much for such sticky affection. Let those who can only hate go on hating; but let them know that the man they hated was big enough to have for them almost as much casual contempt as he would have had for that other slack-jawed lot of shrine-worshipers.

One says farewell to the *years* of Roosevelt, for they have in any case irrecoverably gone. But there is no farewell now, and never will be, to all that he was and did and caused, this singular breaker of the whole long rope of time.

In this sense, when one looks back from the aftertime, it is clear now he was the first President of a new America changed wholly and forever—not merely in degree but also in kind— from all the Americas that had gone before him.

The true, the real Roosevelt Revolution lay not in what was called the New Deal; it lay instead in what was in fact a totally new form of management of a nation, a new and enduring method of political leadership, a new way of national life, involving a curiously practical merger of public compassion and private selfishness, which set the country upon paths which never before had it trod.

Who speaks of the consequences of the Roosevelt era must speak first of all of an era that has not ended, and will not. There is no past tense here; for though a man has departed a state of affairs remains. And who speaks of consequences must speak deepest of all of a series of fundamental convulsions, as real as earthquakes below the surface, in the whole of the American society, political, economic, social, which might be said to have ushered in a wholly new phase of history.

Everything that since has happened in public affairs may be traced, with a singular clarity, to what had happened in his time and tenure, sometimes by his design, more often without his conscious plan or purpose.

But was he not often a seemingly divisive leader? Yes, he was; but the divisions which occurred at the visible level of American life would turn out to be trifling and passing, against the supreme fact which lay underneath: that he had, at its core, drawn the American life more together in truth than it had ever been—more together perhaps in some ways than it should be—in an unexampled victory for human Average which, while rightfully and largely destroying Subaverage had also ill-served occasional Excellence.

For the long phase of the Frontier in America, which had persisted from George Washington all the long way through Herbert Hoover, had died before Franklin Roosevelt, the first of what will now be a long series of modern Presidents, had himself died. It is in fact a farther true distance, except in the merest of chronological measures, from Coolidge to Roosevelt than it had been from Coolidge all the way back to Madison—or even Jefferson.

So goodbye to Roosevelt, the man. But who can say goodbye to Roosevelt, the symbol? Who can say goodbye to something that has not gone and will not go?

Index